HUXTABOOK

RECIPES
FROM
SEA, LAND
& EARTH

•

DANIEL
WILSON

•

hardie grant books

HUXTABOOK

INTRODUCTION

From a young age I loved eating. I guess the natural progression from there was to learn to cook delicious food. I was always amazed how raw ingredients could combine to become such delicious meals. My favourite part of Saturday morning kids' shows was always the cooking segments, I even wrote in a few times to get the recipes, including one for French toast that I still use!

DAN'S BEEN COOKING SINCE HE WAS 5 YEARS OLD.

My approach to cooking is to use the best possible ingredients to produce great yet uncomplicated food. This is where Huxtable comes in. I met Dante and Jeff, my business partners, upon moving to Melbourne in 1998. We became good friends — they were bartenders, and I was a thirsty chef on the other side of the bar; I was full of energy, wanting to learn everything. We kept in touch over the years as we each worked in various restaurants around Melbourne and overseas.

In early 2010 the idea for Huxtable was born. We came together with the idea to start a restaurant that was comfortable, with delicious but simple food, an excellent wine list and attentive yet relaxed service. We did as much work as we could to help the builders, even painting digging trenches and.

HE ALSO RUNS HUXTABURGER ACROSS THE ROAD.

Huxtable has given me the opportunity to truly express my own style of cooking. The response has been absolutely fantastic, and we have such a great following from both locals and diners from afar.

The recipes that follow are mostly designed for sharing, as I feel this is the best way to eat. Food is to be shared, and enjoyed with loved ones. I believe there is no better way to connect with family and friends than over a great meal with delicious wine.

I hope you can try these recipes without fear, and share the result with those you cherish. Just remember that recipes are not set in stone (except maybe fancy pastry stuff) and that if you don't like an ingredient, you can substitute it. Use this book as a guide for flavour, but don't feel bound by the rules. Let your senses deliver a delicious result for your loved ones!

HUXTABLE

DANIEL WILSON

MAP OF CONTENTS

BITES

12. Crisp filo logs of lamb puttanesca with lemon yoghurt
14. Crumbed oysters with pickled plum tartare
15. Tom yum school prawns
16. Quail terrine with golden raisin relish
19. XO buns with crab & jalapeño & Thai basil mayo
20. Fennel-cured salmon with cucumber & lemon crème fraîche
22. Olive-crumbed basil mozzarella with smoked tomato sauce
23. Jalapeño & cheddar croquettes
26. Tempura eggplant & prawn fritters with shiso
27. Cured ocean trout with black vinegar & ginger
28. Rice flour-crusted oyster po' boy with sriracha mayo
30. Foie gras parfait with croutons & pickled figs
33. Steamed crab & corn rice noodle rolls with XO chilli sauce
34. Steamed tofu with chilli, ginger & black bean dressing
35. Steamed tofu with sesame spinach & soy daikon
36. Southern fried chicken ribs & jalapeño mayo
38. Chilli smoked mussels with aïoli & pickled shallot
41. Stilton & quince oatcake oreos

SEA

44. Lightly smoked kingfish with horseradish cream, baby beetroot, pear & kombu
46. John dory with clams, buttered leek & saffron
47. King salmon sashimi with fresh wasabi, yuzu & sesame dressing
48. King prawn salad with chilli pineapple, bean sprouts & red curry dressing
50. Dashi-poached eggs with confit salmon & sesame spinach
53. Ceviche of scallops, octopus & snapper with chilli & lime
54. Tuna with Japanese flavours & tempura crumbs
56. Rice-crusted snapper with green papaya, chilli & peanut salad
58. Ocean trout with harissa, beetroot & avocado
59. Bonito with crème fraîche, pickled shallot, apple & fennel
60. Kingfish sashimi with pear kimchi, wakame & sesame
63. Seared ocean trout with piperade basquaise & lemon
64. Snapper with sichuan eggplant & pickled cucumber
65. Spiced tuna tartare with shiso, yuzu custard, radish & rice crackers
68. Steamed cod with Asian mushrooms, tofu, wakame & sesame
71. Coconut prawn salad with rice noodles, lychees & cashew praline
72. Hot smoked barramundi with apple kimchi, miso dressing & baby cos
74. Spicy dory with sichuan eggplant & mushroom & garlic chips
75. Smoked eel with apple jelly, pink fir potatoes & horseradish
77. Crisp king salmon tail with pomelo, peanut & chilli salad
78. John dory with fricassée of peas, smoked mussels & lomo

LAND

82. Korean barbecued pork ribs with spicy slaw & chilli gherkins
85. Veal tartare with soft-boiled egg & brioche soldiers
86. Roasted duck breast with sautéed red cabbage, quince purée & hot mustard
88. Fried duck eggs with chilli-braised ham hock & pickled okra
90. Grass-fed porterhouse with caramelised onion purée & pepper sauce
92. Wagyu & green peppercorn curry with coconut, shallot & lime leaf
93. Pork schnitzel with sesame, plum tonkatsu, yuzu mustard & dashi mushrooms
94. Chargrilled quail with prosciutto & peach & witlof salad
96. Red wine braised beef short ribs with parsnip purée & persillade
100. Smoked pork cheek with coconut sauce, finger lime & lychees
102. Rare sesame beef salad with lemongrass, lime, peanuts & rice paddy herb
103. Five-spice crispy quail with green mango salad, radish & cashews
104. Roasted duck breast with pickled cherries, hazelnut quinoa & herbed goat's curd
106. Wagyu beef tataki with roasted shallot & chilli dressing & toasted rice

EARTH

SWEET

BASICS

INDEX

BITES

CRISP FILO LOGS OF LAMB PUTTANESCA WITH LEMON YOGHURT

- 1 boneless lamb or mutton shoulder, about 1.5 kg (3 lb 5 oz)
- 1 kg (2 lb 3 oz/4 cups) tinned whole tomatoes, crushed with your hands
- 155 g (5½ oz/1 cup) pitted kalamata olives
- 6 anchovy fillets
- 12 garlic cloves
- 3 tablespoons salted capers, rinsed
- 2 long red chillies, sliced into rounds
- 10 basil stems, leaves finely chopped
- 375 g (13 oz) packet kataifi pastry (shredded filo), left in the packet at room temperature for about 1 hour
- melted ghee (clarified butter), for brushing

LEMON YOGHURT

- 1 kg (2 lb 3 oz/4 cups) Greek-style yoghurt
- juice of 2 lemons

Essentially a fancy sausage roll, these have been on the menu since day one. The richness of the lamb is perfectly cut with the freshness of the lemon yoghurt. Prepare the lamb and lemon yoghurt a day ahead.

FOR THE LEMON YOGHURT

Line a sieve with muslin (cheesecloth) and set it over a bowl. Put the yoghurt in the sieve and leave to drain overnight in the fridge. The next day, mix the lemon juice through and season with sea salt and freshly ground black pepper. Refrigerate until ready to use, but bring to room temperature for serving.

FOR THE LAMB

Preheat the oven to 110°C (230°F). Line a roasting tin with baking paper. Trim any large pieces of fat from the outside of the shoulder, but don't remove all. Season the lamb with salt and pepper, then place it in the roasting tin. Spread the tomatoes, olives, anchovies, garlic, capers and chilli over the lamb, then wrap well with foil. Bake for 10 hours, or overnight.

When the meat is done, transfer the meat and other bits to a colander set over a bowl. Once the meat has cooled a little, but is not cold, pick it apart with your fingers and discard any fatty bits. Mix the meat well with all the olives, garlic and other bits.

Once the juices have settled, transfer them to a saucepan, skim off the excess fat, then reduce the liquid over high heat for 20 minutes, until thick. Mix the liquid through the meat mixture, then add the basil. Check the seasoning: it may need some pepper, but should be salty enough from the capers and olives.

Line a 25 cm x 30 cm (10 inch x 12 inch) dish with baking paper. Press the lamb mixture into the dish, so it's about 1.5 cm (½ inch) thick. Place another piece of baking paper on top, then a flat tray roughly the same size. Top with some weight, such as a few tins of food. Refrigerate for at least 4 hours, until firm.

FOR THE LOGS

Cut the meat mixture into 24 logs. Tease the kataifi pastry strands apart with your fingers. Lay a portion of the pastry on the bench, in a rectangle shape, and brush liberally with melted ghee. Put a meat log on top, and roll the pastry around it. Place on a baking tray lined with baking paper and repeat with the remaining pastry and meat. Refrigerate for 20 minutes to allow the ghee to set.

Preheat the oven to 190°C (375°F). Bake the logs for 10 minutes, turning once. Serve warm, with the lemon yoghurt on the side.

MAKES 24 LOGS

CRUMBED OYSTERS WITH PICKLED PLUM TARTARE

- vegetable oil, for deep-frying
- 1 egg
- 125 ml (4 fl oz/½ cup) milk
- 120 g (4½ oz/2 cups) panko breadcrumbs (see Note on page 93)
- 12 oysters, shucked and dried on paper towel
- plain (all-purpose) flour, for dusting
- 1 tablespoon dried wakame, blitzed in a coffee grinder to a powder

PICKLED PLUM TARTARE

- 250 g (9 oz/1 cup) Japanese mayonnaise (kewpie)
- 2 tablespoons white miso paste
- 2 tablespoons diced umeboshi (Japanese pickled plums)
- 2 tablespoons mirin
- 2 spring onions (scallions), finely sliced
- 1 teaspoon Japanese mustard (see Note), or other strong mustard
- 1 tablespoon pickled ginger, finely diced, plus 3 teaspoons juice from the pickled ginger

Oysters are often a polariser. Some love them and some hate them. I personally love them and feel the best way to enjoy them is with a very simple squeeze of lemon or a touch of mignonette sauce. We are lucky to have amazing Pacific oysters from Tasmania, and Sydney rock oysters, but I would have to say that my favourite oysters are from Smoky Bay in South Australia. Plump and briny, they make you feel like you've just dived through a wave. During winter you might find these crumbed oysters on the menu at Huxtable ...

FOR THE PICKLED PLUM TARTARE

Mix together all the ingredients and set aside.

FOR THE OYSTERS

Heat about 2.5 cm (1 inch) of vegetable oil in a saucepan to 180°C (355°F). Test by dipping a wooden chopstick into the oil: the chopstick will sizzle when the oil is ready.

Whisk together the egg and milk. Place the breadcrumbs in a bowl.

Dust the oysters with the flour, then coat in the egg wash, then the breadcrumbs. Put the oysters back into the egg wash, then back into the breadcrumbs, to double-crumb them.

Gently lower the oysters into the hot oil and cook for 3 minutes, or until golden brown. Remove from the oil with a slotted spoon and drain on paper towel.

Serve straight away in a bowl, sprinkled with the wakame powder, and with the tartare sauce on the side for dipping.

MAKES 12

JAPANESE MUSTARD, OR KARASHI, IS A BLEND OF GROUND MUSTARD SEEDS AND HORSERADISH. YOU CAN FIND IT AT MOST ASIAN GROCERS, SOLD EITHER AS A POWDER OR IN A TUBE AS A PASTE.

TOM YUM SCHOOL PRAWNS

— 1 litre (34 fl oz/4 cups) vegetable oil, for deep-frying
— 150 g (5½ oz/1 cup) plain (all-purpose) flour
— 1½ tablespoons lemongrass powder
— 1½ tablespoons kaffir lime (makrut) leaf powder
— 1 tablespoon chilli powder
— 1 tablespoon galangal powder
— 2 teaspoons garlic powder
— 500 g (1 lb 2 oz) school prawns (small shrimp)

School prawns — little bite-sized prawns — are best fried and eaten whole. The are wild caught in many parts of Australia, but are mostly sold frozen. They have a short shelf life and are best cooked the day they are thawed. Here they are tossed in a flour mixture seasoned with the flavours of Thai tom yum soup.

In a medium-sized saucepan, heat the oil to 180°C (355°F). Test by dipping a wooden chopstick into the oil: the chopstick will sizzle when the oil is ready.

Mix the flour with the spice powders. Toss the prawns in the flour mixture, then place in a sieve and shake off the excess flour.

Gently lower the prawns into the hot oil and cook for 90 seconds, or until crisp. Remove using a slotted spoon and drain on paper towel.

Season with sea salt and serve immediately, with beer!

SERVES 4 AS A SNACK OR STARTER

QUAIL TERRINE WITH GOLDEN RAISIN RELISH

- 50 ml (1¾ fl oz) Cognac
- 2 bay leaves, cut into thirds
- 2 thyme sprigs, picked and chopped
- 200 g (7 oz) minced (ground) fatty pork
- 200 g (7 oz) minced (ground) veal
- 2 garlic cloves, lightly bruised with a knife
- 2 scant teaspoons sea salt
- pinch of curing salt (see Note)
- pinch of quatre épices (see Note)
- 2 tablespoons shelled pistachio nuts, toasted
- 3 jumbo quails, flat boned (see method on page 94)
- olive oil, for brushing
- salt flakes, for sprinkling
- cornichons, to serve
- sourdough croutons, to serve

RAISIN RELISH

- 100 g (3½ oz) golden raisins
- 75 ml (2½ fl oz) sherry vinegar

In a bowl, mix together the Cognac, bay leaves, thyme, pork, veal, garlic and a pinch of freshly ground black pepper. Cover and refrigerate for at least 2 hours.

Remove the garlic cloves and bay leaves. Mix in the salt, curing salt, quatre épices and pistachios.

You now need to work the proteins and emulsify the mixture, to make a forcemeat stuffing, or 'farce'. You can do this using the paddle attachment of an electric mixer on a fairly high speed, or by mixing vigorously with one hand and repeatedly slapping the farce against the side of the bowl. Keep the mixture as cold as possible at all times, otherwise it can split and will go grainy and dry when cooked.

Lay out two layers of plastic wrap on your bench. Lay the boned quails out flat next to each other, with the skin side underneath. Make a long sausage out of the farce, then place it along the bottom third of each quail. Roll up, using the plastic wrap to help you, then roll until the quail are completely sealed. Grab the plastic at each end, then roll it back on the bench a couple of times to tighten the roll. Tie the excess plastic wrap into a knot at each end, keeping it as tight as possible at all times.

Bring a large saucepan of water to poaching temperature (just below simmering point — there should be no movement in the water, maybe just a few bubbles on the bottom of the pan). Add the wrapped terrine and poach for 45 minutes, or until firm and cooked through. Remove from the water and leave to rest for 10 minutes at room temperature, then place in an iced water bath to cool.

CURING SALT CONTAINS SODIUM NITRITE (AND SOMETIMES SODIUM NITRATE) AND IS USED FOR PRESERVING MEAT SMALLGOODS.

QUATRE ÉPICES, OR 'FOUR SPICES', IS A FRENCH SPICE MIX OF WHITE PEPPER, CLOVES, NUTMEG AND GINGER, OFTEN USED IN TERRINES.

FOR THE RAISIN RELISH

Place the raisins and vinegar in a small saucepan with 75 ml (2½ fl oz) water and cook over medium heat for 15 minutes, or until the raisins are soft and plump, and most of the liquid has evaporated. Purée until very smooth, then season with sea salt and freshly ground black pepper. Pass through a fine sieve and set aside. The relish can be refrigerated in a clean airtight jar for up to 1 month; bring to room temperature for serving.

TO SERVE

Using a sharp knife, and leaving the plastic on to keep its round shape, thinly slice the terrine, then remove the plastic and arrange the slices on a platter. Brush the top of each slice with olive oil and sprinkle with salt flakes. Serve the raisin relish, cornichons and croutons on the side.

SERVES 6 AS A SNACK OR STARTER

RAISIN
RELISH

QUAIL
TERRINE

SOURDOUGH
CROUTONS

THAI BASIL
MAYO

XO BUNS WITH CRAB & JALAPEÑO & THAI BASIL MAYO

- 120 g (4½ oz) blue swimmer crabmeat, cooked and meat picked
- lime juice, to taste

XO BUNS

- 240 g (8½ oz) plain (all-purpose) flour
- 1 heaped teaspoon sea salt
- 2 teaspoons sugar
- 125 ml (4 fl oz/½ cup) milk
- 2 teaspoons (7 g) dried yeast
- 1 egg
- 20 g (¾ oz) butter, softened
- 1 heaped tablespoon XO chilli sauce (page 184)

GLAZE

- 1 egg yolk
- 3 teaspoons milk

JALAPEÑO & THAI BASIL MAYO

- 2 fresh jalapeño chillies, seeded
- 1 handful picked Thai basil
- pinch of citric acid
- 500 g (1 lb 2 oz/2 cups) Japanese mayonnaise (kewpie)

For these soft little buns we have taken the idea of brioche, and replaced some of the butter with one of my favourite Asian sauces. The fresh, spicy crabmeat enlivens the richness of the bun. The mayo can be made a day ahead, but the buns are best enjoyed the same day.

FOR THE XO BUNS

Place the flour, salt and sugar in the bowl of an electric mixer with a dough hook attached.

In a saucepan, heat the milk and 30 ml (1 fl oz) water to lukewarm, then whisk in the yeast.

Add the yeast mixture and egg to the flour mixture. Beat for 1 minute at medium speed, then slowly add the butter and XO chilli sauce. Knead using the dough hook for 8 minutes. Remove the dough from the bowl and cover with plastic wrap. Leave to prove in a warm, draught-free area for 1 hour, or until doubled in size.

Lightly knock back the dough, then roll into 12 balls. Cover with a clean cloth and leave to prove again for 30–45 minutes, or until doubled in size.

Meanwhile, preheat the oven to 190°C (375°F).

Place the dough balls on a baking tray. Mix together the glaze ingredients, then brush over the buns. Bake for 10 minutes.

FOR THE JALAPEÑO & THAI BASIL MAYO

Place all the ingredients in a food processor and purée. Pass through a sieve and set aside. (You'll have more mayo than you need, but it goes with pretty much everything, so simply refrigerate any leftovers and use as desired; it will keep well for up to 1 week.)

TO SERVE

Warm the buns in a preheated 160°C (320°F) oven, then slice in half.

While the buns are warming, mix the crabmeat with enough mayo so that it is nicely coated, but not sloppy. Season with lime juice and sea salt and freshly ground black pepper.

Place about 1½ tablespoons of the crab mixture on each bottom bun and replace the lids. Serve immediately.

MAKES 12 BUNS

FENNEL-CURED SALMON WITH CUCUMBER & LEMON CRÈME FRAÎCHE

- 220 g (8 oz/1 cup) table salt
- 220 g (8 oz/1 cup) sugar
- 50 ml (1¾ fl oz) gin
- 1 fennel bulb, chopped
- zest of 1 lemon
- 1 x 500 g (1 lb 2 oz) skinless salmon fillet, bloodline removed
- lemon-infused extra virgin olive oil, for drizzling
- dill sprigs, to garnish

PICKLED CUCUMBER

- 1 telegraph (long) cucumber, peeled and seeded, flesh diced into 5 mm (¼ inch) cubes
- 100 ml (3½ fl oz) chardonnay vinegar
- pinch of sea salt

LEMON CRÈME FRAÎCHE

- 125 g (4½ oz/½ cup) crème fraîche
- zest and juice of 1 lemon

This is the perfect starter for a summer dinner with friends. Enjoy with a glass of riesling or pinot gris to get your palate excited for the coming meal.

FOR THE PICKLED CUCUMBER

Combine the ingredients in a non-metallic bowl. Cover and leave to marinate in the fridge for 6 hours, or overnight.

TO CURE THE TROUT

Blitz the salt, sugar, gin, fennel and lemon zest in a food processor. The mixture will be a little wetter than most dry cures, so don't be alarmed.

Put half the mixture on a plate lined with plastic wrap. Place the fish on top, then cover with the remaining cure mixture. Bring the sides of the plastic up to cover the fish and make a little parcel. Refrigerate for 6 hours.

FOR THE LEMON CRÈME FRAÎCHE

Whisk together the ingredients until thick. Season with sea salt and freshly ground black pepper and set aside.

TO SERVE

Remove the fish from its parcel and wash off the cure mixture. Pat the fish dry with paper towel. Using a sharp knife, cut the fish into 5 mm (¼ inch) slices and arrange on a plate or platter.

Drizzle lemon olive oil over the fish, then arrange the cucumber around evenly. Pipe or spoon little dots of lemon crème fraîche whimsically over and around the salmon. Garnish with dill sprigs and serve.

SERVES 4

PIPE OR SPOON LITTLE
DOTS OF LEMON
CRÈME FRAÎCHE
WHIMSICALLY
OVER AND AROUND
THE SALMON

OLIVE-CRUMBED BASIL MOZZARELLA WITH SMOKED TOMATO SAUCE

— 2 eggs
— 250 ml (8½ fl oz/1 cup) milk
— 12 basil mozzarella 'knots'; alternatively, use small plain mozzarella or bocconcini, make a slit in each one and insert a basil leaf in each slit
— plain (all-purpose) flour, for dusting
— snipped basil cress, to garnish

OLIVE CRUMBS

— 155 g (5½ oz/1 cup) pitted kalamata olives
— 160 g (5½ oz/2 cups) fresh breadcrumbs

SMOKED TOMATO SAUCE

— 3 teaspoons olive oil
— 1 French shallot, sliced
— 4 garlic cloves, chopped
— 400 g (14 oz) tin San Marzano tomatoes (see Note), or other sweet, good-quality tinned tomatoes, broken up with your hands
— smoked salt (see Note), to taste

We have a great relationship with Kirsty from La Latteria, a 'mozzarella laboratory' just around the corner from Huxtable. She makes these wonderful little hand-tied 'knots' of mozzarella studded with basil. aten with the olive crumbs and smoked tomato sauce they kind of taste like pizza!

FOR THE OLIVE CRUMBS

Dehydrate the olives for 1½–2 hours in a preheated 120°C (250°F) oven, or for 6–8 hours in a food dehydrator, until the olives are very dry. Blitz the dried olives in a food processor with the breadcrumbs until you have fine black crumbs. Store in an airtight container for up to 3 days.

FOR THE SMOKED TOMATO SAUCE

Heat the olive oil in a small saucepan and sweat the shallot and garlic over medium heat until soft, but without colour. Add the tomatoes and cook for 15 minutes, or until the sauce starts to thicken. Blitz with a hand blender, then pass through a fine sieve to remove the seeds. Season to taste with smoked salt and freshly ground black pepper.

TO CRUMB THE MOZZARELLA

Combine the eggs and milk in a bowl. Place the olive crumbs in another bowl. Dust the mozzarella knots with flour, dredge them through the egg wash, then coat in the olive crumbs. Put the mozzarella knots back into the egg wash, then back into the breadcrumbs, to double-crumb them. Squeeze the crumbs on firmly to make sure there aren't any holes when cooking.

TO SERVE

Heat about 5 cm (2 inches) of vegetable oil in a large saucepan to 180°C (355°F). Test by dipping a wooden chopstick into the oil: the chopstick will sizzle when the oil is ready.

Working in three batches, deep-fry the mozzarella knots 2–3 minutes, until the crumbs are crisp. Be careful, as the cheese inside will become runny and molten, and if you leave the balls in there too long they'll explode! Remove from the oil using a slotted spoon and drain immediately on paper towel.

Serve on a platter, garnished with basil cress, with a bowl of smoked tomato sauce on the side.

MAKES 12

• SAN MARZANO IS A SWEET, LOW-ACID ITALIAN ROMA (PLUM) TOMATO VARIETY.

• SMOKED SALT ADDS A SMOKY FLAVOUR TO DISHES, WITHOUT ALL THE EFFORT. YOU'LL FIND IT IN SPICE SHOPS.

JALAPEÑO & CHEDDAR CROQUETTES

- 250 ml (8½ fl oz/1 cup) milk
- 35 g (1¼ oz) butter, diced
- 65 g (2¼ oz) plain (all-purpose) flour
- 1½ tablespoons cornflour (cornstarch)
- 40 g (1½ oz/⅓ cup) chopped pickled jalapeño chillies
- 50 g (1¾ oz) grated cheddar
- vegetable oil, for deep-frying

CRUMBING MIXTURE

- 2 eggs
- 250 ml (8½ fl oz/1 cup) milk
- 160 g (5½ oz/2 cups) fresh breadcrumbs
- plain (all-purpose) flour, for dusting

These little guys have been probably the most popular bite at Huxtable. They're inspired by an American bar snack called the jalapeño popper (a whole jalapeño chilli stuffed with cheese, then crumbed and fried). Ours are creamy in texture and do really scream for beer! One is never enough.

FOR THE CROQUETTES

Combine the milk, butter, flour and cornflour in a saucepan. Cook over medium heat, stirring constantly, for about 15 minutes, until the sauce is very thick and the floury taste has cooked out. Make sure the sauce is very thick, otherwise you won't be able to roll and crumb the croquettes.

Spoon the mixture into a bowl. Add the jalapeños and cheese and season with sea salt and freshly ground black pepper. Refrigerate for at least 4 hours, until firm.

TO CRUMB THE CROQUETTES

Whisk together the egg and milk. Place the breadcrumbs in a bowl.

Roll the cold cheese mixture into 12 balls. Dust the balls with the flour, then coat in the egg wash, then the breadcrumbs. Put the croquettes back into the egg wash, then back into the breadcrumbs, to double-crumb them.

Place on a tray lined with plastic wrap, then refrigerate for about 1 hour to set the crumbs.

TO SERVE

Heat about 5 cm (2 inches) of vegetable oil in a large saucepan to 180°C (355°F). Test by dipping a wooden chopstick into the oil: the chopstick will sizzle when the oil is ready.

Working in batches, deep-fry the croquettes for 1–2 minutes, or until golden. Remove from the oil using a slotted spoon and drain immediately on paper towel.

Season with sea salt and enjoy hot, with a frosty beer.

MAKES 12

TEMPURA
EGGPLANT

JALAPEÑO
& CHEDDAR
CROQUETTES

CHILLI GARLIC
DIPPING SAUCE

OLIVE-CRUMBED
BASIL MOZZARELLA

PUT OUT A BUNCH
OF SMALL FORKS SO
GUESTS CAN GRAZE

TEMPURA EGGPLANT
& PRAWN FRITTERS WITH SHISO

— 2 long thin eggplants
  (aubergine), sliced diagonally
  into ovals 3 mm (⅛ inch) thick
— vegetable oil, for deep-frying
— 400 g (14 oz) packet tempura
  batter flour
— plain (all-purpose) flour,
  for dusting

CHILLI GARLIC DIPPING SAUCE

— 2 garlic cloves, sliced
— 2 red bird's eye chillies, sliced
— 50 g (1¾ oz) palm sugar
  (jaggery), chopped
— 100 ml (3½ fl oz) fish sauce
— 100 ml (3½ fl oz) lime juice

PRAWN MOUSSE

— 1 kg (2 lb 3 oz) tiger prawn
  (shrimp) cutlets (see Note),
  tails removed
— 1 egg white
— 1 tablespoon soy sauce
— 3 teaspoons sesame oil
— 3 teaspoons fish sauce
— 6 spring onions (scallions),
  sliced
— 2 tablespoons chopped
  coriander (cilantro)
— 2 tablespoons black sesame
  seeds, toasted
— 2 tablespoons white sesame
  seeds, toasted
— 6 shiso leaves, sliced
  (see Note)

These little light and crispy fritters of fried prawn mousse are another crowd favourite. The sweetness of the prawn with the hot, salty, garlic, fishy, sour dressing is hard to resist.

FOR THE CHILLI GARLIC DIPPING SAUCE

Finely blitz the garlic, chilli and palm sugar in a food processor. Add the fish sauce and lime juice and blitz again until the sugar has dissolved. Transfer to a small serving bowl and set aside.

FOR THE PRAWN MOUSSE

Blitz the prawns in a food processor until smooth. Slowly add the egg white, soy sauce, sesame oil and fish sauce while the motor is running. The mixture should be light and fluffy.

PRAWN CUTLETS HAVE THE HEAD AND VEIN REMOVED; THE BODY IS ALSO PEELED, LEAVING THE SHELL ON THE VERY TAIL OF THE PRAWN, REDUCING PREPARATION TIME.

Transfer the prawn mixture to a bowl and fold the remaining mousse ingredients through. The mousse is best made only when you are ready to assemble the fritters, otherwise it will set and will not be very pliable.

FOR THE FRITTERS

Lay half the eggplant slices on a chopping board or tray lined with baking paper. Place a ping-pong ball sized piece of prawn mousse on each one, then top with another piece of eggplant. Cover and refrigerate until ready to cook.

TO COOK

Heat about 10 cm (4 inches) of vegetable oil in a large saucepan to 180°C (355°F). Test by dipping a wooden chopstick into the oil: the chopstick will sizzle when the oil is ready.

SHISO, ALSO CALLED PERILLA, IS A MEMBER OF THE MINT FAMILY. IT HAS A SLIGHTLY CITRUSY, CUMIN FLAVOUR AND IS WIDELY USED IN JAPAN AND KOREA.

Meanwhile, make the tempura batter according to the method on the packet.

Roll each fritter in plain flour, then completely cover them in the batter. Working in batches, gently slide the fritters into the hot oil. Cook for 2–3 minutes on each side, or until puffed and golden. Remove from the oil using a slotted spoon and drain immediately on paper towel.

Serve hot, with the dipping sauce on the side.

MAKES 16 FRITTERS

CURED OCEAN TROUT WITH BLACK VINEGAR & GINGER

— 1 x 250 g (9 oz) skinless ocean trout fillet, bloodline removed
— 100 ml (3½ fl oz) Chinese black vinegar
— 50 ml (1¾ fl oz) light soy sauce
— 2 cm (¾ inch) knob fresh ginger, peeled and grated
— 3 tablespoons grated daikon (white radish)
— snipped coriander (cilantro) cress, to garnish

Chinese black vinegar is a rich, aged, malty vinegar, made from rice and sometimes other grains. I like to think of it as being like an Asian balsamic or malt vinegar, yet earthier and not as sweet. Here, the vinegar and ginger are the perfect foil for the fattiness of the ocean trout. Try to get the belly part of the fish if possible.

Cut the ocean trout into 12 portions of equal size.

Mix together the vinegar, soy sauce and ginger, then strain out and discard the ginger fibres.

Mix the ocean trout with the dressing and leave to cure for 10 minutes.

Remove the trout from the curing mixture and place on a platter. Top each portion with a small ball of grated daikon and a few sprigs of coriander cress.

SERVES 12

RICE FLOUR-CRUSTED OYSTER PO' BOY WITH SRIRACHA MAYO

- 4 small Vietnamese bread rolls
- 125 g (4½ oz/½ cup) Japanese mayonnaise (kewpie)
- 3 teaspoons sriracha chilli sauce (see Note)
- vegetable oil, for deep-frying
- 12 oysters, shucked and washed in salted water to remove any shell
- rice flour, for dusting
- ½ iceberg lettuce, finely sliced

As I did my formal chef training in the United States, I'm well versed in the many different sandwiches they make there. These were one of the first po' boys to appear on a Melbourne menu, and they have now popped up in lots of places around town. I find them especially good when nursing a hangover.

Slice the bread rolls in half, leaving one side intact, and warm them in a moderate oven.

Mix the mayonnaise with the chilli sauce.

Heat about 5 cm (2 inches) of vegetable oil in a large saucepan to 180°C (355°F). Test by dipping a wooden chopstick into the oil: the chopstick will sizzle when the oil is ready.

Dust the oysters in the rice flour and lower them into the hot oil. Deep-fry for 1 minute, or until just cooked through and crisp. Remove from the oil using a slotted spoon and drain immediately on paper towel.

Toss the lettuce through the mayo chilli dressing and place inside the warm buns. Top each bun with three oysters and enjoy!

MAKES 4

SRIRACHA CHILLI SAUCE IS A THAI SAUCE MADE FROM CHILLIES, VINEGAR, GARLIC, SUGAR AND SALT. MOST ASIAN GROCERS STOCK IT.

TOP EACH BUN
WITH THREE OYSTERS
AND TUCK IN

FOIE GRAS PARFAIT WITH CROUTONS & PICKLED FIGS

— 1 sourdough baguette
— mustard cress, to garnish

FOIE GRAS PARFAIT

— 125 ml (4 fl oz/½ cup) port
— 100 ml (3½ fl oz) Madeira
— 1 French shallot, finely diced
— 1 garlic clove, finely chopped
— 3 thyme sprigs, picked and chopped
— 375 g (13 oz) duck livers, trimmed and roughly chopped
— 155 g (5½ oz) unsalted butter, melted and cooled
— 100 g (3½ oz) foie gras, diced, at room temperature
— 1 egg
— 1½ teaspoons sea salt

PICKLED FIGS

— 4 figs, halved
— 75 ml (2½ fl oz) merlot vinegar

FOR THE FOIE GRAS PARFAIT

Preheat the oven to 120°C (250°F).

Place the port, Madeira, shallot, garlic and thyme in a small saucepan. Simmer over medium heat for 5 minutes, or until the mixture is reduced to almost dry. Leave to cool.

Place the livers in a small non-stick frying pan and stir over medium heat for 30 seconds on each side, or until they just start to change colour. Transfer to a food processor. Add the port mixture, melted cooled butter, foie gras, egg and sea salt and season with freshly ground black pepper. Process until the mixture is smooth, then strain through a fine sieve set over a bowl. Using a spatula, push the mixture through the sieve, discarding any solids.

Spray a 750 ml (25½ fl oz/3 cup) mould with cooking oil spray, then line with two layers of plastic wrap, being sure to smooth out any air bubbles or creases. Pour the parfait mixture into the mould, then place in a roasting tin. Pour enough boiling water into the roasting tin to come one-third up the side of the mould.

Transfer to the oven and bake for 45 minutes, or until the parfait is just set. Remove the mould from the water bath and cool to room temperature, then cover with plastic wrap and refrigerate overnight, or until chilled and firm.

FOR THE PICKLED FIGS

Place the fig halves in a bowl with the vinegar and some freshly ground black pepper and gently mix together. Cover and leave to pickle in the fridge for at least 24 hours, or up to 2 days.

Strain and drain on paper towel before use. Cut each fig half into four pieces.

FOR THE CROUTONS

Preheat the oven to 160°C (320°F). Slice the bread into 20 rounds, about 3 mm (⅛ inch) thick. Place on a baking tray and bake for about 10 minutes, or until crisp. Leave to cool, then store in an airtight container until required.

TO SERVE

Smear a generous amount of parfait onto each crouton. Top with the figs, garnish with mustard cress and serve.

MAKES 20

PICKLED FIGS

SMEAR A
GENEROUS
AMOUNT
OF PARFAIT
ONTO EACH
CROUTON

TOP WITH THE
XO CHILLI SAUCE

SERVE WARM,
STRAIGHT FROM
THE STEAMER

STEAMED CRAB & CORN RICE NOODLE ROLLS WITH XO CHILLI SAUCE

— 1 x 175 g (6 oz) packet rolled Vietnamese rice noodles (ban cuon; these are rolled up in logs)
— 120 g (4½ oz) blue swimmer crabmeat, cooked and meat picked
— 1 banana leaf portion, for serving the noodle parcels
— XO chilli sauce, to serve (page 184)
— snipped coriander (cilantro) cress, to garnish

CORN PURÉE

— 4 cobs sweet corn
— 1 egg, lightly beaten
— 1 tablespoon chopped coriander (cilantro)

These delicious little parcels are a delight for the mouth and were inspired by my annual trips to Asia. The soft chewy noodle with the sweet crabmeat and silky texture of the sweet-corn custard is perfect with the luxurious XO chilli sauce. They are quite a bit of work to produce, but well worth it.

FOR THE CORN PURÉE

Grate the corn, then place in a heatproof bowl with the egg. Set the bowl over a saucepan of simmering water, ensuring the base of the bowl does not touch the water. Cook, stirring constantly, for about 10 minutes, or until the mixture is thick and no longer runny.

Pass the mixture through a fine strainer. Season with sea salt and freshly ground black pepper and leave to cool. The purée can be made a day ahead; refrigerate in an airtight container and mix in the coriander just before using.

TO MAKE THE ROLLS

Cut the rolled noodles into 12 sections about 3 cm (1¼ inches) long. Place several noodle portions in a bamboo steamer lined with baking paper. Set the steamer over a saucepan or wok of rapidly boiling water. Cover with the steamer lid and steam for about 1 minute, or until the noodles are just soft enough to unroll. Remove from the steamer and set aside while steaming the remaining noodle portions.

Place a good smear of the corn purée on each noodle length, then put 2 teaspoons of the crabmeat on top of each. Roll up and place on a tray. You can now refrigerate the rolls for up to 1 day to steam later, or steam and serve straight away.

TO SERVE

Working in batches, place the noodles in a bamboo steamer lined with baking paper. Set the steamer over a saucepan or wok of rapidly boiling water. Cover with the steamer lid and steam for 3–4 minutes, or until heated through.

Arrange on a platter and serve straight away, topped with XO chilli sauce and garnished with coriander cress.

MAKES 12

STEAMED TOFU WITH CHILLI, GINGER & BLACK BEAN DRESSING

- 1 x 375 g (13 oz) block organic firm tofu
- snipped coriander (cilantro) cress, to garnish

CHILLI, GINGER & BLACK BEAN DRESSING

- 75 ml (2½ fl oz) peanut oil
- 2 cm (¾ inch) knob fresh ginger, peeled and julienned
- 2 French shallots, finely sliced
- 2 garlic cloves, julienned
- 1 long red chilli, halved, seeded and julienned
- 3 tablespoons salted black beans, soaked in water and drained
- 3 teaspoons light soy sauce

Tofu is an interesting ingredient. On its own it doesn't taste like much, but it's great for taking on other flavours. We use organic tofu from a local company called Earnest Bean. This recipe and the one that follows are two different ways to dress up simple steamed tofu.

FOR THE CHILLI, GINGER & BLACK BEAN DRESSING

Heat the peanut oil in a saucepan over medium heat and add the ginger, shallot, garlic and chilli. Cook over low heat for 15 minutes, stirring occasionally, until the ingredients all start to soften and come together.

Stir in the black beans and soy sauce and cook for another 5 minutes. Remove from the heat and allow to cool.

TO SERVE

Cut the tofu into 12 pieces of the same size. Working in batches if necessary, place the tofu in a bamboo steamer lined with baking paper. Set the steamer over a saucepan or wok of rapidly boiling water. Cover with the steamer lid and steam for 4–5 minutes, or until the tofu is heated through.

As soon as the tofu comes out of the steamer, place about 2 teaspoons of the dressing on top of each portion.

Garnish with coriander cress and serve immediately.

MAKES 12 SERVES

STEAMED TOFU WITH SESAME SPINACH & SOY DAIKON

— 1 x 375 g (13 oz) block organic firm tofu

SESAME SPINACH

— 80 g (2¾ oz/½ cup) sesame seeds, toasted
— 40 g (1½ oz/¼ cup) peanuts, roasted
— 3 teaspoons soy sauce
— 3 teaspoons mirin
— 1 teaspoon sugar
— 1 teaspoon finely grated fresh ginger
— 500 g (1 lb 2 oz) baby English spinach, washed

SOY DAIKON

— 1½ tablespoons light soy sauce
— 60 ml (2 fl oz/¼ cup) untoasted sesame oil
— 1 teaspoon ginger juice (made by grating and squeezing peeled fresh ginger)
— 1 teaspoon lime juice
— 1 small daikon (white radish)

FOR THE SESAME SPINACH

Place all the ingredients, except the spinach, in a food processor. Blitz to make a smooth dressing.

Blanch the spinach for 30 seconds in a large saucepan of salted boiling water. Drain the spinach and refresh immediately in iced water. Remove thespinach from the iced water and squeeze to remove the excess moisture.

Just before serving, mix enough of the dressing through the spinach to coat it well.

FOR THE SOY DAIKON

In a bowl, mix together the soy sauce, sesame oil, ginger juice and lime juice to make a dressing.

Peel the daikon, then julienne using the fine blade on a Japanese mandoline. Toss the daikon with the dressing until well coated.

TO SERVE

Cut the tofu into 12 pieces of the same size. Working in batches if necessary, place the tofu in a bamboo steamer lined with baking paper. Set the steamer over a saucepan or wok of rapidly boiling water. Cover with the steamer lid and steam for 4–5 minutes, or until the tofu is heated through.

As soon as the tofu comes out of the steamer, place some soy daikon on each portion, then top with a mound of sesame spinach. Serve immediately.

MAKES 12 SERVES

SOUTHERN FRIED CHICKEN RIBS & JALAPEÑO MAYO

— 500 ml (17 fl oz/2 cups) buttermilk, or 500 ml (17 fl oz/2 cups) milk mixed with 1 tablespoon lemon juice
— 1 kg (2 lb 3 oz) chicken ribs, trimmed of excess fat
— vegetable oil, for deep-frying

JALAPEÑO MAYO

— 150 g (5½ oz) Japanese mayonnaise (kewpie)
— 2 tablespoons jalapeño chilli sauce, or to taste

SPICED FLOUR

— 1 teaspoon cayenne pepper
— 1 teaspoon ground turmeric
— 3 teaspoons sweet paprika
— 2 teaspoons sea salt
— 3 teaspoons ground cumin
— 1 teaspoon Chinese-five spice
— 3 teaspoons ground coriander
— 2 teaspoons garlic powder
— 2 teaspoons onion powder
— 3 teaspoons ground sichuan peppercorns
— 2 teaspoons ground white pepper
— 150 g (5½ oz/1 cup) plain (all-purpose) flour

These deliciously moreish snacks are sure to go down a treat; served cold they also make excellent picnic fare. The spiced flour mix is also great dusted on seafood before cooking.

FOR THE RIBS

Place the buttermilk in a large bowl or dish and add the ribs. Cover and refrigerate overnight. Soaking the ribs in the buttermilk tenderises the chicken and makes it extra juicy.

FOR THE JALAPEÑO MAYO

Whisk together the mayonnaise and jalapeño chilli sauce and set aside. You can add more or less chilli sauce depending on how spicy you like it.

FOR THE SPICED FLOUR

Mix all the ingredients together in a bowl.

TO COOK

Heat about 5 cm (2 inches) of vegetable oil in a large saucepan to 180°C (355°F). Test by dipping a wooden chopstick into the oil: the chopstick will sizzle when the oil is ready.

Remove the chicken ribs from the buttermilk in small batches. Toss well through the spiced flour, then shake off the excess using a sieve.

Gently lower the ribs into the oil and cook for 2–3 minutes, or until golden and crisp. Drain immediately on paper towel.

TO SERVE

Simply spread the mayonnaise out in a circle on a plate, then pile the hot chicken on top.

SERVES 4

SPREAD THE MAYO IN
A CIRCLE ON A PLATE,
THEN PILE THE HOT
CHICKEN ON TOP

CHILLI SMOKED MUSSELS WITH AÏOLI & PICKLED SHALLOTS

- 3 teaspoons olive oil
- 1 French shallot, sliced
- 1 garlic clove, sliced
- 1 kg (2 lb 3 oz) mussels, hairy beards removed, scrubbed well
- wood chips, for smoking
- snipped coriander (cilantro) cress, to garnish
- Aïoli (page 178), to serve

PICKLED SHALLOTS

- 4 French shallots, sliced into thin rounds using a mandoline
- 1 teaspoon sea salt
- 125 ml (4 fl oz/½ cup) chardonnay vinegar
- 55 g (2 oz/¼ cup) sugar

CHILLI PASTE

- 50 ml (1¾ fl oz) olive oil
- 2 long red chillies, halved and seeded, flesh side grated
- 2 garlic cloves, grated
- 2 cm (¾ inch) knob fresh ginger, peeled and grated

I love mussels, pickled shallots and aïoli, so this dish is a no-brainer. The smoking adds another dimension to the sweet mussels. Such a good snack or starter.

Heat the olive oil in a saucepan over high heat. Add the shallot and garlic and cook for 1 minute. Now add the mussels, stir and cover. Let the mussels steam in their own juices for 2 minutes, or until they have all opened. Discard any that haven't opened.

Strain the mussels and place them on a tray to cool down.

FOR THE PICKLED SHALLOTS

Toss the shallots with the salt in a non-reactive heatproof bowl. Bring the vinegar and sugar to the boil, then pour over the shallots. Cover with plastic wrap and allow to cool. Strain the shallots and set aside. Keep in an airtight container until required; the pickled shallots will keep in the fridge for up to 1 week.

FOR THE CHILLI PASTE

Heat the olive oil in a small non-stick sauté pan over low heat. Add the chilli, garlic, ginger and a pinch of sea salt. Cook, stirring frequently, for 10 minutes, or until the mixture has lost its raw taste. Remove from the heat and allow to cool. (The chilli paste can be made a day ahead.)

TO SMOKE THE MUSSELS

Heat the wood chips in a smoker or kettle barbecue until they start to smoke. (Alternatively, line the bottom of an old wok or saucepan with foil, place your wood chips on the foil and heat over a high gas flame until smoking.)

Remove the mussels from their shells and check for any beards you may have missed. Mix the mussels with the chilli paste and place on a rack that will fit into your smoking device. Reduce the heat to low, cover and leave to smoke for 30–40 minutes, depending on how smoked you'd like the mussels. Remove from the smoker and allow to cool.

TO SERVE

Arrange the mussels on a plate and scatter with the pickled shallot and coriander cress. Serve the aïoli in a bowl on the side for dipping.

SERVES 4

SCATTER WITH
PICKLED SHALLOT AND
CORIANDER CRESS

SERVE WITH
AÏOLI FOR
DIPPING

SMOKING
ADDS ANOTHER
DIMENSION
TO THE SWEET
MUSSELS

STILTON & QUINCE OATCAKE OREOS

— 150 g (5½ oz) Stilton, at room temperature
— 150 g (5½ oz) quince paste

OATCAKES

— 150 g (5½ oz) oatmeal
— 80 g (2¾ oz) butter, diced
— 50 g (1¾ oz/⅓ cup) plain (all-purpose) flour
— 2 tablespoons brown sugar
— ½ teaspoon bicarbonate of soda (baking soda)

These are a great way to end a meal and are a lovely alternative to a cheese plate. I believe that Stilton is one of the best cheeses in the world. The combination of the cheese, quince paste and crumbly oatcakes is a winner.

FOR THE OATCAKES

Preheat the oven to 175°C (345°F). Line a large baking tray with baking paper.

Place all the ingredients in a food processor with a pinch of sea salt and blend until well combined. Turn out onto a lightly floured bench, add a little cold water and lightly knead to form a dough.

Roll the dough out to 3 mm (⅛ inch) on a lightly floured surface. Cut out 24 rounds, using a 4 cm (1½ inch) cutter, and place on the baking tray.

Bake for 12–15 minutes, or until lightly golden. Remove from the oven and leave to cool.

Store in an airtight container for up to 2 days.

TO ASSEMBLE

Roll the Stilton between two sheets of baking paper to about 3 mm (⅛ inch) thick. Chill for 15 minutes, or until firm.

Cut out 12 circles of cheese, using a 4 cm (1½ inch) cutter. Place each one on the flat side of a biscuit.

Cut the quince paste into 12 slices about 3 mm (⅛ inch) thick, then cut into rounds using the 4 cm (1½ inch) cutter. Place over the Stilton rounds.

Top with the remaining oatcakes, placing them flat side down, and serve.

MAKES 12

LIGHTLY SMOKED KINGFISH WITH HORSERADISH CREAM, BABY BEETROOT, PEAR & KOMBU

— wood chips, for smoking
— 500 g (1 lb 2 oz) skinless kingfish or tuna fillet, pin boned and bloodline removed
— 1 pear
— 1 sheet shaved kombu (see Note)
— snipped red sorrel cress, to garnish

BEETROOT

— 6 red baby beetroot (beets)
— 6 golden baby beetroot (beets)
— 6 candy-stripe baby beetroot (beets)
— 150 ml (5 fl oz) white wine vinegar
— 150 g (5½ oz) sugar
— 3 teaspoons black peppercorns
— 3 bay leaves
— 150 ml (5 fl oz) chardonnay vinegar
— 150 ml (5 fl oz) extra virgin olive oil

HORSERADISH CREAM

— 250 g (9 oz/1 cup) quark
— 2 tablespoons grated fresh horseradish

This is a very pretty dish with clean flavours. Kingfish responds very well to cold smoking — perfectly complemented by the sweetness of the beetroot and the spiciness of the horseradish. If you can't find quark (a soft fresh cottage cheese), crème fraîche will do.

TO SMOKE THE FISH

Heat the wood chips in a smoker or kettle barbecue until they start to smoke. (Alternatively, line the bottom of an old wok or saucepan with foil, place your wood chips on the foil and heat over a high gas flame until smoking.) Put the cold fish on an oiled rack that will fit into your smoking device. Cover, reduce the heat to low and leave to smoke for 30 minutes.

Remove the fish from the smoker and immediately return to the fridge.

FOR THE BEETROOT

Trim the stalks off the beetroot. Wash the beetroot well under cold running water. Place each beetroot variety in a separate saucepan and cover with water. Add 50 ml (1¾ fl oz) of the white wine vinegar, 50 g (1¾ oz) of the sugar, 1 teaspoon of the peppercorns, a bay leaf and a pinch of sea salt to each pan. Bring to a gentle boil and cook over medium heat for about 20 minutes, or until just tender. Drain. While the beetroot are still warm, slip off the skins (wearing latex gloves). Cut into halves, or quarters if large, then toss with the chardonnay vinegar, olive oil and some salt and freshly ground black pepper. Set aside.

FOR THE HORSERADISH CREAM

Mix the quark and horseradish together and season to taste. Set aside.

TO SERVE

Slice the fish across the bias. Smear the horseradish cream across one side of individual plates or a large platter. Twirl the fish slices into small 'cones' and spread evenly on the cream.

Place the different coloured beetroot around the fish, on the cream. Cut the pear into thin 'matchsticks' and lean them up against the fish at different angles. Break the kombu into smaller ribbons and drape over the dish. Garnish with the sorrel leaves and serve.

SHAVED KOMBU IS A SEAWEED THAT IS FERMENTED, DRIED, THEN THINLY SHAVED. IT HAS A 'UMAMI' FLAVOUR AND MELTS IN THE MOUTH. YOU'LL FIND IT IN HEALTH FOOD STORES AND ASIAN GROCERS.

SERVES 4 AS PART OF A SHARED MEAL

USE BOTTLED HORSERADISH
IF YOU CAN'T GET FRESH
HORSERADISH

SEA

JOHN DORY WITH CLAMS, BUTTERED LEEK & SAFFRON

- 50 ml (1¾ fl oz) olive oil
- 2 French shallots, sliced
- 2 garlic cloves, sliced
- 1 kg (2 lb 3 oz) diamond-shell clams (vongole), or other fresh clams
- 100 ml (3½ fl oz) riesling
- 3 leeks, white part only
- 100 g (3½ oz) butter, plus an extra 50 g (1¾ oz) diced cold butter
- decent pinch of good-quality saffron
- 100 g (3½ oz) ghee (clarified butter)
- 500 g (1 lb 2 oz) skinless john dory fillets; alternatively, you could use halibut or perch
- 1 handful roughly chopped flat-leaf (Italian) parsley

This dish is so rich and comforting. The not-so-secret ingredient that makes it luxurious is butter! The briny flavour of the clams and the acidity of the wine pair perfectly with the sweet fish and saffron. This is definitely a dish to have a crusty sourdough loaf nearby for! I prefer the amazing New Zealand diamond-shell clams for this dish, but you can use whatever fresh clams you can get your hands on.

Heat a saucepan over high heat and sauté the olive oil, shallot and garlic. Sauté for 1 minute, then add the clams and riesling, stir, and put a lid on. Cook for 2–3 minutes, or until the clams have all opened.

Drain the clams into a colander set over a bowl; discard any unopened clams, but reserve the clam juice. Leave the clams to cool for 5 minutes, then remove the clams from their shells. Strain the clam juice through a coffee filter, then add the clams back to the liquid so they stay plump and juicy.

Slice the leeks in half lengthways. Wash out any dirt or sand by holding the top of the leeks under running water, facing the sink, so that you don't wash any dirt back inside the leek. Cut the leeks into 1 cm (½ inch) cubes.

Heat a wide-based non-stick saucepan over low heat and add the 100 g (3½ oz) butter. Add the saffron, then the leek, then cook for about 15 minutes, until the leek is just soft. Add the clams and clam juice and cook for another 5 minutes. Season with sea salt and freshly ground black pepper.

Meanwhile, heat a large non-stick frying pan over medium–high heat and add the ghee. Season the fish with salt and pepper, then cook for 3 minutes on each side, or until just cooked through and slightly golden on the outside.

TO SERVE

Stir the parsley through the clams; add the cold, diced butter and stir until melted and emulsified. Check the seasoning and spoon into a large, wide bowl.

Top with the fish fillets and serve with a decent chardonnay. Don't forget the crusty bread for dipping.

SERVES 4 AS PART OF A SHARED MEAL

KING SALMON SASHIMI WITH FRESH WASABI, YUZU & SESAME DRESSING

— 1 x 400 g (14 oz) skinless sashimi-grade king salmon fillet, pin boned and bloodline removed
— 2 tablespoons wasabi furikake
— snipped purple daikon cress, to garnish
— snipped green daikon cress, to garnish

WASABI, YUZU & SESAME DRESSING

— 50 ml (1¾ fl oz) white soy sauce
— 25 ml (¾ fl oz) yuzu juice (see Note)
— 1 tablespoon grated fresh wasabi
— 50 ml (1¾ fl oz) untoasted virgin sesame oil

The softness of the king salmon provides a really wonderful sashimi mouthfeel. The very simple dressing goes beautifully with the fish, while the furikake offers a bit of crunch and 'umami'. Furikake is a Japanese seasoning mixture that is often sprinkled over rice. There are many varieties, but most contain seaweed, dried fish and sesame seeds. Wasabi furikake simply has wasabi in the mix. It is available from Asian grocery stores.

FOR THE WASABI, YUZU & SESAME DRESSING

Using a sharp knife, cut the salmon across the grain, into slices about 3 mm (⅛ inch) thick. Arrange nicely on a platter.

Combine all the dressing ingredients in a bottle, seal the lid and shake well.

TO SERVE

Drizzle the dressing directly over and around the salmon. Sprinkle with the furikake and garnish with the purple and green daikon cress.

Serve the sashimi nice and cold!

SERVES 4 AS PART OF A SHARED MEAL

YUZU IS A KIND OF JAPANESE CITRUS FRUIT. THE JUICE IS SOLD IN BOTTLES AT GOOD JAPANESE GROCERS. BE CAREFUL WHEN ADDING BOTTLED JUICE TO DISHES, AS IT IS SOMETIMES SALTED.

KING PRAWN SALAD WITH CHILLI PINEAPPLE, BEAN SPROUTS & RED CURRY DRESSING

- — 1 mature coconut, opened, peeled and grated
- — 8 Thai basil stems, picked
- — 6 mint sprigs, picked
- — 1 handful picked coriander (cilantro)
- — 250 g (9 oz) bean sprouts, washed
- — 2 red Asian shallots, finely sliced
- — 2 red bird's eye chillies, halved, seeded and cut into half-rounds
- — 2 kaffir lime (makrut) leaves, very finely sliced
- — 1 banana leaf square, wiped with a damp cloth, for serving

CHILLI PINEAPPLE

- — 1 just-ripe pineapple (a little green is okay)
- — 1 teaspoon chilli powder
- — 1 tablespoon sea salt

POACHED PRAWNS

- — 1 whole lemongrass stem, bruised
- — 50 ml (1¾ fl oz) fish sauce
- — 2 kaffir lime (makrut) leaves
- — 12 raw king prawns (shrimp), peeled and deveined, leaving the tails intact

RED CURRY DRESSING

- — 1 tablespoon vegetable oil
- — 2 kaffir lime (makrut) leaves
- — 2 tablespoons red curry paste
- — 50 g (1¾ oz) chopped palm sugar (jaggery)
- — 400 ml (13½ fl oz) coconut milk
- — 50 ml (1¾ fl oz) fish sauce
- — 50 ml (1¾ fl oz) lime juice

This is a perfect summer seafood salad. The pineapple is tossed with a little salt and chilli powder, which is how they serve a lot of fruit in Thailand. Use the best-quality prawns you can, so their flavour really shines through.

FOR THE CHILLI PINEAPPLE

Cut the pineapple into four quarters, then cut away the peel and core. Cut the flesh into 1 cm (½ inch) cubes. Place in a large bowl and sprinkle with the chilli powder and salt. Toss well, cover and macerate in the fridge overnight.

FOR THE POACHED PRAWNS

Half-fill a saucepan with cold water and add the lemongrass, fish sauce and lime leaves. Bring to the boil, then remove the lime leaves and lemongrass. Reduce the heat so the water is just below simmering point, then add the prawns and poach for 3–4 minutes, or until firm and just cooked through.

Remove the prawns from the poaching liquid, place on a tray or plate and immediately place in the fridge. (I prefer not to use an iced water bath to chill the prawns, as this just waters down their flavour and can make them soggy.)

FOR THE RED CURRY DRESSING

Heat a small saucepan over medium heat and add the vegetable oil. Once hot, add the lime leaves and curry paste. Cook for 3–4 minutes, or until fragrant. Add the palm sugar and cook for another 5 minutes.

Stir in the coconut milk until well combined, then simmer for 20 minutes, or until the raw curry taste has cooked out. Remove from the heat, then stir in the fish sauce and lime juice. Set aside and leave to cool.

TO SERVE

In a large mixing bowl, toss together the prawns, chilli pineapple, coconut, herbs, bean sprouts, shallot, chilli and most of the sliced lime leaf. Just before serving, add enough dressing to nicely coat the salad.

Place the banana leaf on a large platter and pile the salad on top, in a nice pyramid-like shape. Garnish with the remaining lime leaf and serve with a crisp riesling or a frosty beer.

SERVES 4 AS PART OF A SHARED MEAL

PERFECT SUMMER
SEAFOOD SALAD

SERVE WITH A CRISP
RIESLING OR
A FROSTY BEER

DASHI-POACHED EGGS WITH CONFIT SALMON & SESAME SPINACH

- 4 x 80 g (2¾ oz) skinless king salmon fillets, pin boned and bloodline removed
- 2 tablespoons olive oil
- smoked salt (see Note, page 22), for sprinkling
- 1 quantity Dashi stock (page 179)
- 8 free-range eggs
- 4 slices sourdough bread, toasted
- butter, for spreading
- coriander (cilantro) cress, to garnish

SESAME SPINACH

- 80 g (2¾ oz/½ cup) sesame seeds, toasted
- 40 g (1½ oz/¼ cup) roasted peanuts
- 1 tablespoon soy sauce
- 1 tablespoon mirin
- 1 teaspoon sugar
- 1 teaspoon finely grated fresh ginger
- 500 g (1 lb 2 oz) spinach, washed, blanched and squeezed dry

The dashi stock deliciously, yet subtly, flavours the eggs during poaching. The combination of the gooey runny yolks, rich salmon and savoury spinach make for a decadent yet healthy breakfast.

FOR THE SESAME SPINACH

Place the sesame seeds, peanuts, soy sauce, mirin, sugar and ginger in a food processor and blitz until smooth. Transfer to a bowl, mix the spinach through and set aside.

FOR THE SALMON

Preheat the oven to 100°C (210°F).

Place the salmon fillets on a baking tray lined with baking paper. Rub the fillets with olive oil and sprinkle with smoked salt. Bake for 8–10 minutes, or until the salmon is warmed through and the flesh has changed colour and firmed up slightly.

FOR THE EGGS

Pour the dashi stock into a saucepan that is taller rather than wide. Bring the stock to poaching temperature (just below simmering point — there should be no movement in the stock, maybe just a few bubbles on the bottom of the pan).

Crack the eggs into a cup, then gently slide them into into the stock. Cook for 3–4 minutes, until the whites are firm, but the yolks are still runny.

Remove the eggs from the stock using a slotted spoon. Drain on paper towel.

TO SERVE

Spread the hot toast with butter and place on warm serving plates. Place a small mound of sesame spinach on one corner of the toast and rest a salmon fillet next to it. Place the eggs on the other end of the toast.

Sprinkle with sea salt and freshly ground black pepper and serve garnished with coriander cress.

SERVES 4

DASHI-POACHED
EGGS

SEA

SESAME
SPINACH

CONFIT
SALMON

GARNISH WITH
CORIANDER CRESS

CEVICHE OF SCALLOPS, OCTOPUS & SNAPPER WITH CHILLI & LIME

— 2 x 200 g (7 oz) octopus tentacles
— 6 scallops
— 1 x 200 g (7 oz) skinless snapper fillet, pin boned
— 1 red Asian shallot, finely sliced
— 1 large handful roughly chopped coriander (cilantro)
— 1 long red chilli, halved, seeded and sliced into half-rounds
— juice of 1 lime
— juice of 1 lemon
— juice of ½ orange
— 1 banana leaf square, wiped with a damp cloth, for serving
— snipped coriander (cilantro) cress, to garnish

I love ceviche — cooking seafood with acid so it stays fresh and light. The way the citrus juices firm up the flesh while adding crisp, fresh vibrancy is truly magical.

Wash the octopus tentacles well under running water. Using a sharp knife, score the skin near the tentacles in a diamond pattern, then pull the skin off using your fingers, starting from the thickest part.

Place the tentacles in a large wide saucepan with 100 ml (3½ fl oz) water and a large pinch of sea salt. Cover and cook over low heat for 45 minutes, or until the tentacles are firm but tender. Drain well, then chill in the fridge. Once cold, slice the tentacles diagonally across the grain.

Meanwhile, wash the scallops in a bowl of salted cold water to make sure there is no sand on them. Using a small sharp knife, remove the tough muscle on the side of each scallop. Slice each scallop into five thin strips along the grain of the fibres. Refrigerate.

Slice the snapper fillet in half lengthways, then cut across the fillet into slices 3 mm (⅛ inch) thick. Place back in the fridge.

Near serving time, place the seafood in a mixing bowl, along with the shallot, coriander and chilli. Add the citrus juices and toss together. Leave to sit for 5 minutes for the juices to start curing the seafood.

Line a bowl or platter with the banana leaf. Pile the seafood salad on top and garnish with the coriander cress.

SERVES 4 AS PART OF A SHARED MEAL

TUNA WITH JAPANESE FLAVOURS & TEMPURA CRUMBS

- 1 x 400 g (14 oz) sashimi-grade tuna loin
- vegetable oil, for brushing and deep-frying
- 60 g (2 oz/½ cup) tempura flour
- snipped daikon cress, to garnish
- snipped coriander (cilantro) cress, to garnish
- snipped shiso cress, to garnish

SOY SESAME DRESSING

- 50 ml (1¾ fl oz) light soy sauce
- 50 ml (1¾ fl oz) untoasted virgin sesame oil
- zest and juice of ½ lime
- 2 cm (¾ inch) knob fresh ginger, peeled and finely grated

I love raw tuna and clean, fresh Japanese flavours. This is my take on healthy fish and chips!

Cut the tuna into three long pieces of equal size. Rub each tuna log with a little vegetable oil and some sea salt and freshly ground black pepper.

Heat a non-stick frying pan over high heat. Add the tuna logs, one at a time, and cook for 10 seconds on each side, except the ends. Immediately place on a tray and return to the fridge. Once cool, wrap tightly with plastic wrap to form a nice round shape, then refrigerate.

Heat about 2.5 cm (1 inch) of vegetable oil in a saucepan to 180°C (355°F). Test by dipping a wooden chopstick into the oil: the chopstick will sizzle when the oil is ready.

Mix the tempura flour to a batter, according to the directions on the packet. Using a fork, drizzle the tempura batter into the oil to make little tempura 'crumbs'. After about 1 minute, or once the crumbs are cooked, remove from the oil using a heatproof sieve and drain on paper towel. Season with sea salt.

FOR THE SOY SESAME DRESSING

Mix all the ingredients together, then pass through a sieve to remove the lime zest and ginger fibres. Set aside.

TO SERVE

Using a sharp knife, and leaving them in the plastic wrap to keep their round shape, cut the tuna logs into slices 5 mm (¼ inch) thick. Remove the plastic and arrange the tuna slices in an overlapping circle on the centre of a platter.

Drizzle the dressing over and around the tuna. Sprinkle the tuna with the tempura crumbs and garnish with the three cresses.

SERVES 4 AS PART OF A SHARED MEAL

DRIZZLE THE
TUNA WITH
DRESSING

SEA

TOP WITH TEMPURA
CRUMBS AND THE
MIXED CRESS

RICE-CRUSTED SNAPPER WITH GREEN PAPAYA, CHILLI & PEANUT SALAD

— 100 g (3½ oz/½ cup) jasmine rice
— peanut oil, for pan-frying
— 1 x 500 g (1 lb 2 oz) snapper fillet, skin on, pin boned

DRESSING

— 2 garlic cloves, sliced
— 2 red bird's eye chillies, sliced
— 50 g (1¾ oz) palm sugar (jaggery), chopped
— 100 ml (3½ fl oz) fish sauce
— 100 ml (3½ fl oz) lime juice

GREEN PAPAYA, CHILLI & PEANUT SALAD

— 1 small green papaya
— 1 large handful roughly torn coriander (cilantro)
— 2 snake beans, cut into 4 cm (1½ inch) lengths
— 4 cherry tomatoes, quartered
— 80 g (2¾ oz/½ cup) roasted peanuts, chopped
— 2 red bird's eye chillies, seeded and finely sliced

One of my favourite Thai salads is 'som tam'. I have eaten it from street carts in Phuket, a garage down a laneway of Koh Phi Phi as well as fancy restaurants. What they all had in common was the fire of the chilli, crunch of the green papaya and the sweet, salty, sour and spice of the dressing. The rice crust on the fish gives a lovely contrast to the delicate flesh.

Fry the rice in a dry non-stick frying pan over low heat, stirring frequently, until the rice turns opaque. Transfer to a food processor and pulse until the rice is ground to a consistency slightly coarser than sand. Set aside.

FOR THE DRESSING

Blitz the garlic, chilli and palm sugar in a food processor until finely ground. Add the fish sauce and lime juice and blitz again until the sugar has dissolved.

FOR THE GREEN PAPAYA, CHILLI & PEANUT SALAD SALAD

Peel the skin off the papaya. Using your peeler, continue to peel off thin slices of the papaya, until you reach the seeds. Stack the papaya slices on top of each other. Using a sharp knife, slice them as finely as possible.

Toss the papaya with the remaining salad ingredients, and enough of the dressing to coat them nicely, using your hand to squash and bruise the ingredients together.

TO SERVE

Preheat the oven to 180°C (355°F).

Heat a little peanut oil in a non-stick ovenproof frying pan over medium–high heat. Season the fish with sea salt, then dip the flesh side in the ground rice and press to coat well. Place in the pan, rice-crusted side down, and cook for about 2 minutes.

Turn the fish onto the flesh side, transfer to the oven and bake for 5 minutes, or until just cooked through.

Place a large mound of the salad on a platter and serve the fish alongside, with the crusted side up.

SERVES 4 AS PART OF A SHARED MEAL

SLICE THE
PEELED PAPAYA
AS FINELY
AS POSSIBLE

OCEAN TROUT WITH HARISSA, BEETROOT & AVOCADO

- 6 baby beetroot (beets), stalks removed, washed well
- 100 ml (3½ fl oz) white wine vinegar
- 55 g (2 oz/¼ cup) sugar
- 1 teaspoon black peppercorns
- 1 bay leaf
- 1 tablespoon chardonnay vinegar
- 2 tablespoons extra virgin olive oil
- 1 avocado
- 60 g (2 oz/¼ cup) plain yoghurt
- pinch of citric acid
- snipped beetroot (beet) cress, to garnish

TROUT

- 200 g (7 oz) skinless sashimi-grade ocean trout, pin boned and bloodline removed
- 1 teaspoon finely diced preserved lemon zest
- 1 tablespoon finely sliced coriander (cilantro)
- 2 teaspoons Harissa (page 180)
- extra virgin olive oil, for drizzling

The richness of the fat in the ocean trout works perfectly with the spicy harissa, mellowed by the avocado and pepped up with the lightly pickled beetroot.

Place the beetroot in a saucepan and cover with water. Add the white wine vinegar, sugar, peppercorns, bay leaf and a pinch of sea salt. Bring to a gentle boil, then cook over medium heat for about 20 minutes, or until just tender, then drain. While still warm, slip off the skins (wearing latex gloves). Toss with the chardonnay vinegar and olive oil, season with sea salt and freshly ground black pepper and set aside.

Peel the avocado and chop the flesh into a food processor. Add the yoghurt and citric acid and season to taste. Blend to a purée. Pass the mixture through a fine sieve and set aside.

FOR THE TROUT

Cut the trout into 5 mm (¼ inch) cubes. Place in a mixing bowl with the preserved lemon, coriander, harissa and a drizzle of olive oil. Mix together and season to taste.

TO SERVE

Scatter the trout on a platter and arrange the beetroot among the trout. Pipe or spoon little dots of avocado around. Garnish with beetroot cress and serve.

SERVES 4 AS PART OF A SHARED MEAL

BONITO WITH CRÈME FRAÎCHE, PICKLED SHALLOT, APPLE & FENNEL

- 500 g (1 lb 2 oz) skinless sashimi-grade bonito fillets, pin boned and bloodline removed
- 100 ml (3½ fl oz) rice vinegar
- 1 pink lady apple
- 100 g (3½ oz) crème fraîche
- lemon-pressed extra virgin olive oil, for drizzling
- dried fennel pollen (see Note), for sprinkling (optional)
- tiny fennel tips, to garnish

PICKLED SHALLOT

- 4 French shallots, finely sliced into rounds, then separated with your fingers
- 100 ml (3½ fl oz) rice vinegar
- 100 g (3½ oz) sugar

Bonito is a wonderful tasting, very affordable and sustainable fish. When fresh, it is absolutely delicious and has a very soft, delicate flesh. In this dish it is very lightly pickled.

FOR THE PICKLED SHALLOT

Put the shallot in a heatproof bowl and sprinkle with a little sea salt. In a small saucepan, bring the vinegar, sugar and 100 ml (3½ fl oz) water to the boil, then pour the liquid over the shallot. Cover with plastic wrap and set aside until cool. Leave to pickle for several hours, or store in the refrigerator for up to 1 week.

FOR THE FISH

Sprinkle the fish with sea salt and leave to sit for 10 minutes. Pour the vinegar onto a tray. Roll the fillets around in the vinegar, then transfer the fish to a clean container and discard the vinegar. Cover the fish and leave in the fridge for at least 2 hours.

TO SERVE

Slice the fish across the grain, on an angle, to give nice slices. Cut very thin slices off the side of the apple, then cut these into very thin 'matchsticks'. Drain the pickled shallot well.

Spread the crème fraîche in a circle over a large platter. Arrange the fish slices all around inside the circumference of the crème fraîche. Top with the pickled shallot. Arrange the apple matchsticks all over the fish, at different angles.

Sparingly sprinkle the fennel pollen over the whole dish, if using (it is quite strong). Finish by placing a few tiny fennel tips around the dish.

SERVES 4 AS PART OF A SHARED MEAL

• DRIED FENNEL POLLEN IS AVAILABLE FROM SPECIALTY FOOD STORES, BUT YOU CAN ALSO MAKE YOUR OWN. IF YOU SEE SOME WILD FENNEL GROWING BY THE SIDE OF THE ROAD, PICK SOME OF ITS BEAUTIFUL YELLOW FLOWERS, DRY THEM IN A WARM SPOT, THEN RUB THE YELLOW POLLEN ONTO SOME BAKING PAPER AND STORE IN AN AIRTIGHT CONTAINER.

KINGFISH SASHIMI WITH PEAR KIM CHI, WAKAME & SESAME

— 1 x 400 g (14 oz) skinless sashimi-grade kingfish fillet, pin boned, bloodline removed
— 1 quantity Wakame & sesame salt (page 183)

KIM CHI

— ½ Chinese cabbage (wombok)
— 1 tablespoon sea salt
— 1 tablespoon sugar
— 10 garlic cloves
— 2 cm (¾ inch) knob fresh ginger, peeled and sliced
— 25 g (1 oz/¼ cup) Korean chilli powder
— 30 ml (1 fl oz) fish sauce
— 30 ml (1 fl oz) light soy sauce
— 4 spring onions (scallions), cut into 2 cm (¾ inch) lengths
— 2 pears, julienned

I love kingfish as sashimi. It has great texture and flavour due to its relatively high fat content. Also I love the spicy refreshing crunch of kim chi. The recipe I use is based on one by David Chang from Momofuku, but I omit the fermented prawn (shrimp) sauce and add pear to keep the kim chi more fresh and less 'in your face'.

FOR THE KIM CHI

Cut the cabbage portion in half lengthways. Cut across each portion, to give 2 cm (¾ inch) pieces. Toss the cabbage in a large bowl with the salt and sugar. Place in a colander set over a bowl and leave in the fridge overnight.

The next day, place the garlic, ginger, chilli powder, fish sauce and soy sauce in a food processor and blitz to a thick paste, adding a little water if necessary.

Mix the paste with the cabbage, spring onion and pear. Place in a container and return to the fridge for at least 1 day. The kim chi will keep for up to 1 month, and will get better with age.

TO SERVE

Cut the fish into slices 4 mm (⅕ inch) thick, then arrange in a line on a plate or platter. Sprinkle a thick line of the wakame salt along the middle of the whole row of fish. Place a mound of kim chi next to the fish; you may need to drain it a little first so the juice doesn't run everywhere!

Encourage your friends to dig in with chopsticks and enjoy with a crisp lager.

SERVES 4 AS PART OF A SHARED MEAL

SEA

PEAR KIM CHI

KINGFISH
SASHIMI

THE TROUT SKIN
SHOULD BE GOLDEN
AND CRISP!

SEARED OCEAN TROUT WITH PIPERADE BASQUAISE & LEMON

— 1 x 300 g (10½ oz) ocean trout fillet, skin on, pin boned
— 2 lemon wedges

PIPERADE BASQUAISE

— 1 red capsicum (bell pepper)
— 1 yellow capsicum (bell pepper)
— 2 tomatoes, blanched and peeled
— 100 ml (3½ fl oz) olive oil, plus extra for brushing
— 2 brown onions, julienned
— 4 garlic cloves, julienned
— 4 thyme sprigs

The simplicity of a perfectly cooked piece of fish with sweet, slow-cooked vegetables is hard to beat. I learned this recipe for piperade basquaise while working at Daniel in New York. It is so versatile and delicious.

FOR THE PIPERADE BASQUAISE

Peel the capsicums using a vegetable peeler. Cut the flesh off the sides, in three or four large pieces from each capsicum, away from the inner seeds. Remove the white ribs from the inside, then thinly slice each capsicum piece lengthways into long strips.

Cut the tomatoes into quarters, then cut the flesh into fillets, away from the seeds and inner core. Thinly slice the fillets.

PIPERADE BASQUAISE IS A SOUTHERN FRENCH STEW OF PEPPERS, ONION, GARLIC, TOMATO AND THYME COOKED SLOWLY IN OLIVE OIL.

Warm the olive oil in a wide-based saucepan over medium–low heat. Add the onion, garlic and thyme, and also a pinch of sea salt to help the onion soften. Cook for about 30 minutes, stirring frequently, until the onion and garlic are very soft but have no colour to them.

Add the capsicum and cook for another 20–30 minutes, until it is very soft. Now add the tomato and cook for about 10 minutes longer.

Season with sea salt and freshly ground black pepper. If planning to use the mixture the following day, leave the thyme sprigs in until you plan to serve it, and gently reheat before serving.

FOR THE TROUT

Preheat the oven to 180°C (355°F).

Heat a non-stick ovenproof frying pan over medium–high heat. Season the fish well with salt and pepper and rub with a little olive oil.

Place the fish in the pan, skin side down, and cook for 4–5 minutes. Transfer the pan to the oven and cook for another 4–5 minutes, or until the fish is medium–rare. Remove from the oven and gently turn the fish over with a spatula. The skin should be golden and crisp.

Spread or pile the warm piperade on the middle of a large plate. Place the fish on top and sprinkle with a little sea salt. Serve with the lemon wedges.

SERVES 4 AS PART OF A SHARED MEAL

SNAPPER WITH SICHUAN EGGPLANT & PICKLED CUCUMBER

- 60 ml (2 fl oz/¼ cup) peanut oil
- 500 g (1 lb 2 oz) eggplant (aubergine), diced
- 2 teaspoons Sichuan spice mix (see below)
- 25 ml (¾ fl oz) light soy sauce
- 25 ml (¾ fl oz) black vinegar
- 1 garlic clove, crushed
- 1 tablespoon toban jiang (chilli bean sauce; see Note)
- 1 teaspoon sugar
- 1 spring onion (scallion), sliced
- 1 x 500 g (1 lb 2 oz) snapper fillet, skin on, pin boned
- snipped coriander (cilantro) cress, to garnish

SICHUAN SPICE MIX

- 1 tablespoon cumin seeds
- 2 teaspoons whole sichuan peppercorns
- 1 dried chilli
- 1 teaspoon sea salt

PICKLED CUCUMBER

- 1 Lebanese (short) cucumber, peeled, seeded and flesh julienned
- 1 garlic clove, finely chopped
- 30 ml (1 fl oz) red vinegar
- ½ teaspoon chiu chow chilli oil (see Note)
- 1 teaspoon sugar

The contrast of the delicately fleshed, crisp-skinned snapper against the soft sweet, sour and spicy eggplant is delicious and so moreish! The pickled cucumber provides crunch, acidity and extra spice.

FOR THE SICHUAN SPICE MIX

Toast all the ingredients together in a dry frying pan over medium heat, stirring frequently, for 4–5 minutes, or until fragrant.

Finely grind or pound the toasted spices, using a spice grinder or a mortar and pestle. Transfer to an airtight container until required. The spice mix will keep for up to 1 month in a cool, dark place.

FOR THE PICKLED CUCUMBER

Combine all the ingredients in a bowl. Cover and leave to pickle for at least 2 hours.

TOBAN JIANG IS THE 'SOUL' OF SICHUAN CUISINE. IT IS A SALTED CHILLI PASTE WITH FERMENTED BROAD (FAVA) BEANS, SOYA BEANS AND RICE.

FOR THE EGGPLANT

Heat the peanut oil in a heavy-based saucepan. Add the eggplant and spice mix and cook over medium–high heat for 5–10 minutes, or until the eggplant is soft. Stir in the soy sauce, vinegar, garlic, toban jiang and sugar. Cook for a further 5 minutes, or until the sauce is thick.

Leave to cool, then stir in the spring onion.

TO SERVE

Cook the snapper skin side down in a hot frying pan over medium–high heat for 5 minutes, or until the skin is crisp and the fish is three-quarters cooked through. Turn the fish over to finish cooking for a further 3–4 minutes.

CHIU CHOW CHILLI OIL ORIGINATED FROM CHIU CHOW IN CHINA. MADE FROM DRIED CHILLIES, GARLIC, SOY AND OIL, IT IS QUITE HOT AND CAN BE USED AS A DIPPING SAUCE.

Place the eggplant in a mound on a large plate or platter, then top with the snapper. Use a fork to make a nice twirl of pickled cucumber and place it on top. Drizzle with some of the cucumber pickling liquid, garnish with coriander cress and serve.

SERVES 4 AS PART OF A SHARED MEAL

SPICED TUNA TARTARE WITH SHISO, YUZU CUSTARD, RADISH & RICE CRACKERS

- 400 g (14 oz) sashimi-grade yellowfin tuna, diced
- 2 tablespoons gojuchang (fermented Korean chilli paste)
- 4 shiso leaves (see Note, page 26), finely sliced
- 1 tablespoon sesame seeds, toasted and ground
- 1 tablespoon peanuts, toasted and ground
- Vietnamese sesame rice crackers (see Note), deep-fried or toasted over a flame until puffed
- 1 radish, julienned
- shiso cress, to garnish

YUZU CUSTARD

- 50 ml (1¾ fl oz) mirin
- 50 ml (1¾ fl oz) yuzu juice
- 50 ml (1¾ fl oz) light soy sauce
- 2 duck egg yolks
- 1 whole duck egg

This is a boldly flavoured tartare, spiked with a Korean fermented chilli paste known as gojuchang, traditionally aged outdoors in large earthen pots. The Vietnamese sesame rice crackers are not the same ones you use for rice paper rolls. They are thicker and are studded with black or white sesame seeds, and sometimes dried shrimp, spring onion (scallion) or even coconut. You will find both ingredients at good Asian grocers.

In a bowl, mix the tuna with the gojuchang, shiso and ground sesame seeds and ground peanuts. Taste for seasoning and add a little sea salt if necessary. Refrigerate until ready to use, but bring to room temperature for serving.

FOR THE YUZU CUSTARD

Whisk all the ingredients together in a heatproof bowl. Set the bowl over a saucepan of simmering water, ensuring the base of the bowl does not touch the water. Cook, stirring constantly with a spatula, for about 10 minutes, or until thick.

Strain through a fine sieve, into a clean bowl. Place a round of baking paper on top, to prevent a skin forming, and leave to cool.

IN VIETNAM, RICE CRACKERS ARE OFTEN EATEN WITH SALADS. TO USE, PUFF THEM IN THE MICROWAVE LIKE POPPADOMS, TOAST OVER AN OPEN FLAME UNTIL PUFFED, OR BREAK INTO PIECES AND DEEP-FRY IN 5 CM (2 INCHES) OF VEGETABLE OIL.

TO SERVE

Spoon the yuzu custard over the bottom of a platter or large bowl. Shape the seasoned tuna into a ball and place on top, in a pyramid shape.

Break up the sesame rice crackers into large shards and arrange around the tuna. Serve garnished with the radish and shiso cress.

SERVES 4 AS PART OF A SHARED MEAL

SPICED TUNA
TARTARE

SHISO

YUZU
CUSTARD

SESAME RICE CRACKERS

STEAMED COD WITH ASIAN MUSHROOMS, TOFU, WAKAME & SESAME

— 500 g (1 lb 2 oz) blue cod fillets, skin on, pin boned
— 1 quantity Wakame & sesame salt (page 183)
— red seaweed, to garnish (optional)

ASIAN MUSHROOMS

— 100 ml (3½ fl oz) vegetable oil
— 2 red Asian shallots, sliced
— 2 cm (¾ inch) knob fresh ginger, peeled and julienned
— 150 g (5½ oz) shiitake mushrooms, stems removed, caps thinly sliced
— 150 g (5½ oz) oyster mushrooms, stems removed
— 150 g (5½ oz) shimeji mushrooms, trimmed
— 150 g (5½ oz) enoki mushrooms, trimmed
— 100 ml (3½ fl oz) Dashi stock (page 179)
— 200 g (7 oz) firm tofu, cut into 16 cubes

Blue cod is a wonderful fish, with its sweet flavour and firmly textured white flesh. Steaming really preserves the flavour and is very healthy too. The mushrooms and tofu add 'umami', while the wakame and sesame contribute a natural seasoning and a nutty taste and aroma.

FOR THE ASIAN MUSHROOMS

Heat the oil in a saucepan over medium heat. Add the shallot and ginger and sweat for 2 minutes, or until translucent. Add the shiitake and oyster mushrooms and cook for 5 minutes.

Add the shimeji and enoki mushrooms and cook for another 5 minutes, then stir in the dashi and turn the heat down to low. Once the liquid starts to become a little thick, turn off the heat.

Gently stir the tofu through, being careful not to break it up.

TO STEAM THE COD

Fill a steamer with water, bring to the boil, then reduce the heat to low.

Cut a sheet of baking paper to go underneath the cod. Season both sides of the cod with sea salt, then place the cod on the baking paper, skin side up. Place in the steamer and cook for 10–12 minutes, or until firm and cooked through.

TO SERVE

Reheat the mushrooms so they are hot. Check the seasoning: if they are too salty, just add a little water. Spoon the mushrooms onto a wide plate that has a lip on it.

Remove the cod from the steamer and use a spatula to place it on top of the mushrooms. Sprinkle generously with the wakame and sesame salt, garnish with seaweed if desired and serve.

SERVES 4 AS PART OF A SHARED MEAL

STEAMING THE COD
PRESERVES FLAVOUR

SERVE ON A
BANANA LEAF,
TOPPED WITH
DRIED CHILLI
STRIPS

COCONUT PRAWN SALAD WITH RICE NOODLES, LYCHEES & CASHEW PRALINE

- 1 coconut, halved, peeled, grated and toasted (see Note)
- 3 tablespoons Cashew praline (see below)
- 400 g (14 oz) Vietnamese rice noodles, blanched and refreshed (see Note)
- 6 mint sprigs, picked
- 1 handful coriander (cilantro) leaves
- 2 red bird's eye chillies, sliced
- 1 pomelo, segmented and separated
- 8 lychees, peeled, stoned and quartered
- 80 ml (2½ fl oz/⅓ cup) lime juice
- fish sauce
- 1 banana leaf square, wiped with a damp cloth, for serving
- thinly sliced long dried red chilli strips, to garnish

CASHEW PRALINE

- 200 g (7 oz) palm sugar (jaggery), roughly chopped
- 80 g (2¾ oz/⅓ cup) caster (superfine) sugar
- 1 red bird's eye chilli
- 1 teaspoon dried shrimp
- 155 g (5½ oz/1 cup) cashew nuts, toasted

POACHED PRAWNS

- 1 whole lemongrass stem, bruised
- 50 ml (1¾ fl oz) fish sauce
- 2 kaffir lime (makrut) leaves
- 12 raw king prawns (shrimp), peeled and deveined

This super summer salad has been very popular at Huxtable, although the fresh chillies surprised some people with their burst of heat. The lychees add a wonderful tropical element.

FOR THE CASHEW PRALINE

In a small saucepan, melt the palm sugar and caster sugar with 50 ml (1¾ fl oz) water over medium heat. Cook for about 10 minutes, or until the mixture is a caramel colour.

Meanwhile, blitz the chilli and dried shrimp in a food processor.

Stir the shrimp mixture and cashews into the caramel. Mix well, then pour out onto a tray lined with baking paper. Allow to cool and harden for at least 30 minutes. Once cool and firm, place in a food processor and pulse to the size of coarse breadcrumbs. Store in an airtight container for up to 1 month.

TO POACH THE PRAWNS

Half-fill a saucepan with cold water and add the lemongrass, fish sauce and lime leaves. Bring to the boil, then remove the lime leaves and lemongrass. Add the prawns and cook for 3–4 minutes, or until firm and just cooked.

Remove the prawns from the poaching liquid, place on a tray or plate and immediately place in the fridge. (I prefer not to use an iced water bath to chill the prawns, as this just waters down their flavour and can make them soggy.)

TO SERVE

Put the coconut, cashew praline, noodles, herbs, chilli, pomelo and lychees in a bowl. Add the lime juice and fish sauce and toss together.

Cut the prawns in half, add to the salad and toss again. Serve on a banana leaf, garnished with dried chilli strips.

SERVES 4 AS PART OF A SHARED MEAL

SEA

• TO TOAST GRATED COCONUT, SPREAD IT OVER A BAKING TRAY LINED WITH BAKING PAPER AND TOAST IN A 160°C (320°F) OVEN FOR 10–15 MINUTES, UNTIL GOLDEN AND SLIGHTLY CRISP.

• TO BLANCH RICE NOODLES, COOK THEM IN A POT OF BOILING WATER FOR 20 SECONDS. DRAIN, RINSE UNDER COLD RUNNING WATER UNTIL COOLED, THEN TOSS WITH A LITTLE VEGETABLE OIL SO THEY DON'T STICK.

HOT SMOKED BARRAMUNDI WITH APPLE KIM CHI, MISO DRESSING & BABY COS

— wood chips, for smoking
— 1 x 500 g (1 lb 2 oz) barramundi fillet, pin boned, skin on
— 2 tablespoons raw coconut sugar (available from health food shops)
— 2 baby cos (romaine) lettuce, outer leaves removed
— 1 quantity Kim chi, prepared as directed on page 60, but using 2 julienned green apples instead of pears
— snipped red sorrel cress, to garnish

MISO DRESSING

— 3 tablespoons white miso paste
— 60 g (2 oz/¼ cup) Japanese mayonnaise (kewpie)
— 50 g (1¾ oz) crème fraîche
— 50 ml (1¾ fl oz) mirin

This was an immensely popular dish when it was on the menu at Huxtable, I think because barramundi is such a great fish! Its fat structure makes it perfect for steaming. The salad components are spicy, rich and refreshing, all at the same time.

Heat the wood chips in a smoker or kettle barbecue until they start to smoke. (Alternatively, line the bottom of an old wok or saucepan with foil, place your wood chips on the foil and heat over a high gas flame until smoking.) Put the barramundi, skin side down, on an oiled rack that will fit into your smoking device. Sprinkle the coconut sugar over the flesh side of the fish. Place the rack of fish in your smoking device and reduce the heat to low. Leave to smoke for 30 minutes.

Meanwhile, preheat the oven to 150°C (300°F) and line a baking tray with baking paper.

Transfer the fish to the baking tray, skin side down. Bake for 10–15 minutes, until just cooked through. Remove from the oven and leave to cool.

Separate the lettuce leaves and wash well. Slice the larger leaves in half, removing the central rib at the same time. Dry well in a spinner or on paper towel. Reserve in the fridge until needed.

FOR THE MISO DRESSING

Whisk all the ingredients together and set aside.

TO SERVE

Remove the skin and bloodline from the barramundi, which should peel away easily. Break the fish into large chunks and place back on the lined tray to warm in the oven.

Chop the kim chi into slightly smaller lengths.

Drizzle some of the dressing on a large plate. Toss the lettuce with some of the remaining dressing and arrange on the plate, with the stalks pointing to the centre. Using a spoon, dot small piles of kim chi on and in between the lettuce.

Arrange the fish nicely around the salad. Scatter with the cress and serve.

SERVES 4 AS PART OF A SHARED MEAL

USING A SPOON,
DOT MOUNDS
OF KIM CHI ON
AND BETWEEN
THE LETTUCE

SPICY DORY WITH SICHUAN EGGPLANT & MUSHROOM & GARLIC CHIPS

— 60 ml (2 fl oz/¼ cup) peanut oil
— 500 g (1 lb 2 oz) john dory fillets, skin on, pin boned
— snipped coriander (cilantro) cress, to garnish

CRISPY GARLIC CHIPS

— vegetable oil, for deep-frying
— 12 garlic cloves, shaved into very thin rounds (a mandoline is good for this)

SICHUAN EGGPLANT & MUSHROOM

— 60 ml (2 fl oz/¼ cup) peanut oil
— 500 g (1 lb 2 oz) eggplant (aubergine), diced
— 150 g (5½ oz) enoki mushrooms, trimmed
— 150 g (5½ oz) shimeji mushrooms, trimmed
— 2 teaspoons Sichuan spice mix (see recipe on page 64)
— 8 garlic shoots, cut into 2 cm (¾ inch) lengths
— 25 ml (¾ fl oz) light soy sauce
— 25 ml (¾ fl oz) black vinegar
— 1 garlic clove, crushed
— 1 tablespoon toban jiang (chilli bean sauce; see Note on page 64)
— 1 teaspoon sugar
— 1 spring onion (scallion), sliced

This is another fish dish using the delicious sichuan eggplant, but with Asian mushrooms in it. The dory has the skin on and is sprinkled with crispy garlic chips also. Serve with steamed rice and green vegetables.

FOR THE CRISPY GARLIC CHIPS

Heat about 5 cm (2 inches) of vegetable oil in a small saucepan to 180°C (355°F). Test by dipping a wooden chopstick into the oil: the chopstick will sizzle when the oil is ready.

Add the garlic and move it around constantly to keep it from burning. When it is golden brown, remove using a slotted spoon, onto paper towel. Slow and steady is the way, otherwise some garlic chips will be burned and the others will be raw. The garlic chips will keep cooking, so pull them out just before you think they're ready. Season with sea salt and set aside.

FOR THE SICHUAN EGGPLANT & MUSHROOM

Heat the peanut oil in a heavy-based saucepan. Add the eggplant, mushrooms and spice mix. Cook for 5–10 minutes, or until the eggplant is soft.

Stir in the garlic shoots, soy sauce, vinegar, garlic, toban jiang and sugar. Cook until the sauce is thick. Leave to cool, then stir in the spring onion.

TO SERVE

Heat the peanut oil in a large non-stick frying pan over medium–high heat. Season the dory with sea salt and a sprinkle of the sichuan spice mix. Place in the pan, skin side down, and cook for 4 minutes, or until the skin is crisp. Turn over and cook for another 2–3 minutes, or until just cooked through.

Spoon the room-temperature eggplant mixture into a bowl, then place the fish on top. Sprinkle with the garlic chips and coriander cress and serve.

SERVES 4 AS PART OF A SHARED MEAL

SMOKED EEL WITH APPLE JELLY, PINK FIR POTATOES & HORSERADISH

— 4 large pink fir potatoes,
   or other sweet waxy potatoes,
   such as kipfler (fingerling)
   or king edward, scrubbed well,
   skin on
— 50 ml (1¾ fl oz) chardonnay
   vinegar
— 150 ml (5 fl oz) extra virgin
   olive oil
— 1 whole smoked eel, about
   400 g (14 oz)
— 1 x 50 g (1¾ oz) fresh
   horseradish root, peeled

APPLE JELLY

— 2 granny smith apples
— 2 gelatine leaves, soaked
   in cold water

Smoked eel can be quite unnerving and fiddly to deal with, given all the little bones, but the result is well worth it. If you can't get pink fir potatoes, use another sweet, waxy variety. Fresh horseradish is essential too.

Bring the potatoes to the boil in a saucepan of salted cold water. Simmer for 30 minutes, or until done. Test by giving a gentle squeeze with your thumb and index finger; the potatoes should 'give' a bit. Drain and place in a colander to cool.

When cool enough to handle but still warm, use a paring knife to peel the potatoes, then slice into discs 1 cm (½ inch) thick. Place in a bowl and pour the vinegar and olive oil over. Season with sea salt and freshly ground black pepper and gently toss together. Set aside to cool and soak up the dressing.

To prepare the eel, cut just behind the head with a filleting knife, until you feel the spine. Run your knife flat against the backbone, all the way down to the tail. Repeat on the opposite side. Next, remove the rib cage: starting in the middle of the fillet, then keeping your knife upwards, cut out the edge of the fillet where the belly is. To remove the skin, place your thumb or index finger in between the fillet and the flesh, working it all the way along to the tail end; the skin should come off quite easily. Turn the fillet over. Check along the middle of the thickest part and remove any pin bones using a pair of tweezers. You now should have two clean fillets! Cut them into 2.5 cm (1 inch) lengths and reserve.

FOR THE APPLE JELLY

Use a juice extractor to juice the apples. Skim and strain the juice, then measure it out. Adjust the amount of gelatine to the amount of juice you have; the ratio is 1 gelatine leaf to 100 ml (3½ fl oz) juice. Spray a plastic takeaway container with cooking oil spray (or use a paper towel dipped in oil), then wipe out with paper towel. Warm up 50 ml (1¾ fl oz) of the juice until you can just hold your finger in it, then stir in the gelatine and dissolve. Strain into the plastic container and place in the fridge for at least 2 hours to set.

Once set, cut the jelly into 1 cm (½ inch) cubes and return to the fridge.

TO SERVE

Arrange the potato slices on a platter. Top some of them with the eel portions, then place cubes of apple jelly in between. Drizzle some vinaigrette from the potatoes over and around the plate. Using a fine grater, such as a microplane, grate the horseradish over the plate.

SERVES 4 AS PART OF A SHARED MEAL

THE SALMON
TAIL BECOMES
SUPER CRISPY
WHEN FRIED

SERVE WITH LIME
TO DRIZZLE OVER

CRISP KING SALMON TAIL WITH POMELO, PEANUT & CHILLI SALAD

— 1 king salmon tail, weighing at least 500 g (1 lb 2 oz)
— 50 ml (1¾ fl oz) fish sauce
— vegetable oil for deep-frying
— 1 lime, cut into 2 cheeks

DRESSING

— 4 thin slices fresh galangal, about 2 cm (¾ inch) round
— 1 tablespoon Thai shrimp paste (gapi; available from Asian grocers)
— 180 g (6½ oz/1 cup) chopped palm sugar (jaggery)
— 60 ml (2 fl oz/¼ cup) fish sauce
— 3 red bird's eye chillies, roughly chopped
— 3 tablespoons grated coconut, lightly toasted (see Note on page 71)
— 1 tablespoon peanuts, toasted
— 45 ml (1½ fl oz) Tamarind water (page 183)

POMELO, PEANUT & CHILLI SALAD

— 1 large pomelo, segmented and broken into small pieces
— 160 g (5½ oz/1 cup) roughly chopped roasted peanuts
— 1 handful picked Thai basil
— 1 handful picked coriander (cilantro)
— 2 red bird's eye chillies, halved, seeded and cut into half-rounds

For this dish we use NZ Ōra king salmon tails, the tails being a by-product of the cutting of salmon cutlets. The skin turns super crispy, like a salmon 'crackling'. The salad features pomelo, which is one of my favourite fruits. I love the way it bursts with flavour in your mouth!

FOR THE DRESSING

Preheat the oven to 175°C (345°F) and line a baking tray with baking paper. Wrap the shrimp paste in foil and place on the baking tray with the galangal slices. Roast for 20–30 minutes, or until the galangal is dry and slightly crisp, and the shrimp paste is dry.

Meanwhile, place the palm sugar in a saucepan with the fish sauce and 60 ml (2 fl oz/¼ cup) water. Warm over medium heat until the sugar has dissolved and starts to become a light syrup consistency. Set aside.

Place the roasted galangal and shrimp paste in a food processor with the chilli, coconut and peanuts. Add a large pinch of sea salt and blitz until finely chopped.

Stir the spice mixture through the cooled palm sugar syrup until combined. Add the tamarind water and mix thoroughly. The dressing should taste sweet, salty, sour and hot! Set aside.

FOR THE SALMON

Wash the salmon under cold running water to remove any slime and loose scales. Pat dry with paper towel. Working from the cut end, cut seven or eight slits, parallel to the line of the cut end, at 1.5 cm (½ inch) intervals, all the way to the tail end. Repeat on the other side of the fish. Rub the tail, including the insides of the cuts, with the fish sauce, then leave to sit for 5 minutes. This will season the fish and help it crisp up during frying.

Heat about 10 cm (4 inches) of vegetable oil in a large saucepan to 180°C (355°F). Test by dipping a wooden chopstick into the oil: the chopstick will sizzle when the oil is ready. Gently lower the salmon tail in and cook for 5–6 minutes, until crispy and slightly undercooked on the bone, when you check inside the slit on the thickest part of the fillet — remember the fish will keep cooking once it is out of the oil. Remove with a large slotted spoon and drain on paper towel.

TO SERVE

Place the salmon tail on a platter. Toss the salad ingredients with the dressing until well coated. Serve alongside the salmon, with the lime cheeks.

SERVES 4 AS PART OF A SHARED MEAL

JOHN DORY WITH FRICASSÉE OF PEAS, SMOKED MUSSELS & LOMO

- 1 tablespoon vegetable oil
- 1 French shallot, sliced
- 2 garlic cloves, sliced
- 1 kg (2 lb 3 oz) mussels, beards removed, scrubbed well
- wood chips, for smoking
- 30 g (1 oz) ghee (clarified butter)
- 500 g (1 lb 2 oz) skinless john dory fillets, pin boned
- sourdough bread, to serve

PEA FRICASSÉE

- 350 g (12½ oz) fresh peas, shelled
- 100 g (3½ oz) lomo (see Note) or Canadian bacon, diced
- 50 g (1¾ oz) butter, diced

John dory is one of my favourite fish. I love how firm and sweet it is, and how it goes a little crispy when pan-fried in ghee. The pea fricassée is also delicious with some chopped flat-leaf (Italian) parsley stirred through at the last minute, when adding the butter.

Heat the vegetable oil in a large saucepan over high heat. Add the shallot and garlic and sweat for 30 seconds. Add the mussels and cook for 3–4 minutes, or until they have all opened. Discard any mussels that haven't opened.

Strain the mussels, reserving the mussel liquid in a wide bowl or tray that will fit inside a smoker. Once the mussels have cooled, check again and remove any beards you might have missed. Remove the mussels from their shells and place them in the reserved cooking liquid so they stay juicy and plump.

Heat the wood chips in a smoker or kettle barbecue until they start to smoke. (Alternatively, line the bottom of an old wok or saucepan with foil, place your wood chips on the foil and heat over a high gas flame until smoking.) Place the bowl or tray of mussels and mussel stock into your smoking device. Reduce the heat to low, cover and leave to smoke for 20–30 minutes, depending on how smoked you'd like the mussels. Remove from the smoker and allow to cool.

LOMO IS THE SPANISH WORD FOR 'LOIN'. HERE WE ARE USING VERY LEAN, DRY-CURED PORK LOIN, RATHER THAN BEEF LOIN.

FOR THE PEA FRICASSÉE

Place the peas and lomo in a saucepan. Add the mussel stock and bring to a simmer. Cook for 3 minutes, or until the peas are almost tender.

Add the mussels and cook until the peas are tender. Stir in the butter. You probably won't need any salt, but maybe a little freshly ground black pepper. Keep warm.

TO SERVE

Heat a large non-stick frying pan over high heat with the ghee. Season the fish with salt and pepper, then cook for 2–3 minutes on each side, or until just cooked through.

Spoon the peas and mussels and their liquid into a wide bowl. Arrange the fish fillets on top. Serve with crusty sourdough, to mop up all the juices.

SERVES 4 AS PART OF A SHARED MEAL

LAND

KOREAN BARBECUED PORK RIBS WITH SPICY SLAW & CHILLI GHERKINS

— 8 pork ribs, with the belly
  still attached, cut into
  2 portions of 4 ribs
— Chilli gherkins (page 178),
  to serve

SPICY SLAW

— ¼ Chinese cabbage (wombok),
  finely sliced
— 1 carrot, finely julienned using
  a mandoline
— 1 small daikon, finely julienned
  using a mandoline
— 2 spring onions (scallions),
  green part only
— 100 g (3½ oz) Japanese
  mayonnaise (kewpie)
— 2 tablespoons sriracha chilli
  sauce (see Note, page 28)

CHILLI PASTE

— 125 g (4½ oz/½ cup)
  gojuchang (Korean chilli paste;
  see introduction on page 65)
— 30 ml (1 fl oz) light soy sauce
— 4 garlic cloves, crushed
— 2 cm (¾ inch) knob fresh
  ginger, peeled and finely grated
— 1 tablespoon sugar
— ½ teaspoon ground white
  pepper

Soft, crisp, fatty, chewy, spicy — these ribs are Huxtable's signature dish! For the restaurant, we cook them overnight in a vacuum-sealed bag at 82°C (180°F), but try this version at home.

Preheat the oven to its lowest setting — 80°C (175°F) would be ideal. Place each set of four ribs in separate oven bags. Remove as much air as possible, then tie up the bags so they are absolutely sealed.

Bring an ovenproof saucepan or casserole dish of water to poaching temperature (just below simmering point — there should be no movement in the water, maybe just a few bubbles on the bottom of the pan). The pan needs to be big enough to hold all the pork, but small enough to fit in your oven with the lid on. Place the bags of pork in the pan. Cover, transfer to the oven and cook for 10 hours, or overnight.

Remove the bags from the pan and let the pork rest for 10 minutes. Place the pork bags in a large iced water bath, until the pork is completely chilled and firm.

Remove the pork from the bags. Gently scrape off the jellied pork juice, then cut into individual ribs. Reserve in the fridge.

FOR THE SPICY SLAW

Place the cabbage, carrot, daikon and spring onion in a bowl of iced water for 30 minutes, so they crisp up. Drain, then spin the vegetables in a lettuce spinner to dry them out. Toss the vegetables with the mayonnaise and sriracha chilli sauce and mix well.

FOR THE CHILLI PASTE

Mix all the paste ingredients together and set aside.

TO SERVE

Preheat the oven to 180°C (355°F) and line a baking tray with baking paper.

Heat a large non-stick frying pan over medium heat. Add the ribs and cook until golden and crisp on all sides. Brush the ribs on the two cut sides with the chilli paste. Place on the baking tray and bake for 5 minutes.

Pile the slaw along one side of a platter. Slice the chilli gherkins lengthways and pile on the platter with the ribs. Get your fingers dirty and enjoy with beer!

SERVES 4 AS PART OF A SHARED MEAL

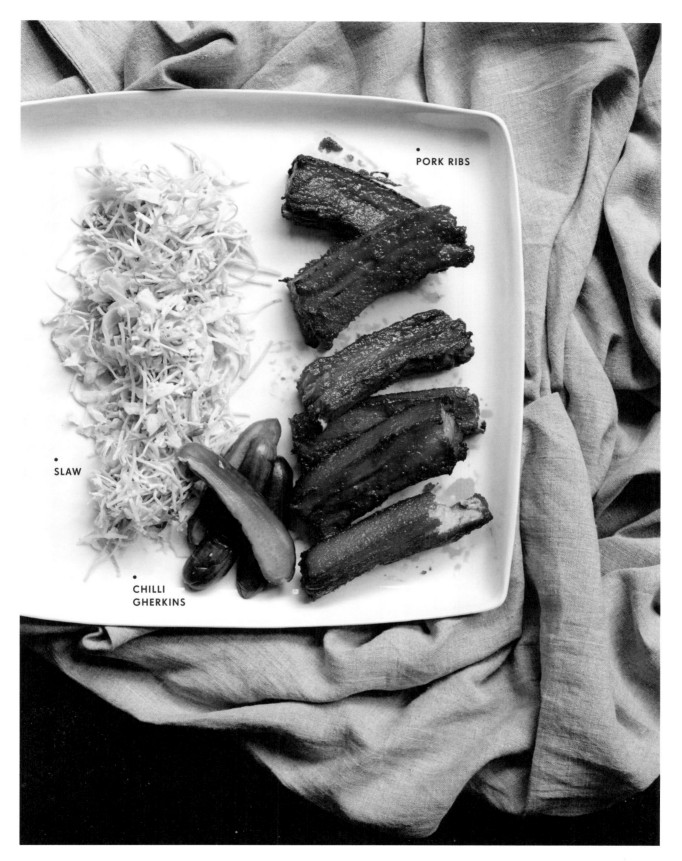

PORK RIBS

LAND

SLAW

CHILLI
GHERKINS

VEAL TARTARE ON
THE OUTSIDE

SOFT-BOILED EGG
ON THE INSIDE

VEAL TARTARE WITH SOFT-BOILED EGG & BRIOCHE SOLDIERS

- 1 free-range egg
- ½ loaf brioche, crusts removed, cut into 2 cm x 2 cm x 6 cm (¾ inch x ¾ inch x 2½ inch) logs
- 150 g (5½ oz) butter, softened
- Tabasco sauce, or other hot pepper sauce, to serve

VEAL TARTARE

- 200 g (7 oz) veal loin, sinew removed, diced into 3 mm (⅛ inch) cubes
- 50 ml (1¾ fl oz) extra virgin olive oil
- 2 tablespoons salted capers, rinsed and chopped
- 2 French shallots, finely diced
- 4 cornichons, finely diced
- 1 tablespoon dijon mustard
- 3 tablespoons finely sliced flat-leaf (Italian) parsley

I think 'tartare' is one of the best ways to eat meat. You can basically flavour it with whatever you like. There's a surprise in the middle of this one — who doesn't like dipping soldiers in some runny egg yolk?

Bring a small saucepan of salted water to the boil. Gently lower the egg in. Cook for 6 minutes, then remove with a slotted spoon and place into an iced water bath. Once cold, peel the egg, being careful to keep it intact. Reserve in the fridge until required.

Preheat the oven to 160°C (320°F) and line a baking tray with baking paper.

Using a pastry brush, coat all sides of the brioche with the butter. Transfer to the baking tray and bake for 10–15 minutes, turning frequently, until golden on all sides. Set aside.

FOR THE VEAL TARTARE

In a bowl, mix all the veal tartare ingredients together until well combined. Season generously with sea salt and freshly ground black pepper. Check the seasoning — the mixture should be very well seasoned as it is served cold.

Pick up the veal mixture in your hand and make a large hole in the middle. Gently poke the whole egg into the hole, then rearrange the meat around the egg to completely cover it.

TO SERVE

Place the veal tartare ball near the middle of a plate, then stack the soldiers alongside. Serve the Tabasco on the side for those who like it hot!

SERVES 4 AS PART OF A SHARED MEAL

ROASTED DUCK BREAST WITH SAUTÉED RED CABBAGE, QUINCE PURÉE & HOT MUSTARD

— 2 x 250 g (9 oz) duck breasts, trimmed of sinew and excess fat
— 2 poached quinces (page 193)

HOT MUSTARD

— 50 g (1¾ oz/¼ cup) brown mustard seeds
— 50 g (1¾ oz/¼ cup) yellow mustard seeds
— 50 ml (1¾ fl oz) port
— 100 ml (3½ fl oz) red wine vinegar
— 1 tablespoon sugar

RED CABBAGE

— 100 g (3½ oz) duck fat
— ½ red cabbage, core removed, finely sliced
— 2 green apples, peeled and grated
— 150 ml (5 fl oz) red wine vinegar
— grated zest of 1 orange

A perfect autumn duck dish. The sweet and sour cabbage and perfume of the quince are saying, 'Crack open a pinot!' Cooking the cabbage in duck fat gives it a lovely savoury element and a great sheen.

FOR THE HOT MUSTARD

Bring all the ingredients to the boil in a small saucepan, then leave to sit at room temperature overnight. Place in a blender and blitz to make a seeded mustard. Season with sea salt and freshly ground black pepper and set aside.

FOR THE DUCK

Preheat the oven to 180°C (355°F). Place the duck on a tray, skin side down. Season the flesh with salt and pepper and rub in well. Using a sharp knife, score the skin in a crisscross pattern.

Cook the duck in an ovenproof frying pan, skin side down, over medium heat for about 5 minutes, until the skin is crisp and golden. Turn the duck over, then transfer the pan to the oven and roast for 4 minutes.

Turn the duck over again and roast for a further 2 minutes. The duck should be somewhere in between medium–rare and medium — rosy but not raw. Place the duck on a rack and leave to rest for at least 10 minutes.

FOR THE QUINCE PURÉE

While the duck is roasting, place the poached quinces in a blender and blitz to a fine purée. Season to taste and set aside at room temperature.

FOR THE RED CABBAGE

While the duck is roasting, heat the duck fat in a wide-based saucepan over medium heat. Add the cabbage and apple and cook down for 8–10 minutes, until the cabbage is wilted and starts to soften. Add the vinegar and orange zest and season with salt and pepper. Cook for a further 10 minutes, or until the mixture is almost dry. Check the seasoning again.

TO SERVE

Reheat the duck breasts in the oven for 5 minutes and make sure the cabbage is hot. Spread the quince purée over a plate or bowl and place the cabbage on top. Slice each duck breast lengthwise into four pieces, sprinkle with a little sea salt and arrange over the plate. Serve the mustard on the side.

SERVES 4 AS PART OF A SHARED MEAL

CRACK OPEN
A PINOT!

LAND

THE DUCK
SHOULD BE ROSY,
BUT NOT RAW

FRIED DUCK EGGS WITH CHILLI-BRAISED HAM HOCK & PICKLED OKRA

- 1 free-range ham hock
- 2 teaspoons chiu chow chilli oil (see Note on page 64)
- 30 ml (1 fl oz) vegetable oil
- 4 duck eggs
- snipped coriander (cilantro) cress, to garnish
- crusty bread, to serve

PICKLED OKRA

- 100 ml (3½ fl oz) rice vinegar
- 1 tablespoon sea salt
- 2 tablespoons sugar
- pinch of mustard seeds
- 1 bay leaf
- 4 okra

SICHUAN SALT & PEPPER

- 2 tablespoons sea salt
- 2 tablespoons whole sichuan peppercorns

I love the marriage of bacon and eggs. This is my version of that combination, with some of my other favourite things including chilli oil, sichuan pepper and pickles. Not for the faint hearted, but rewarding for those who dare!

FOR THE PICKLED OKRA

Bring the vinegar, salt, sugar, mustard seeds and bay leaf to the boil in a small saucepan. Place the okra in a heatproof glass or ceramic bowl, then pour the hot pickling liquid over. Cover while hot and leave to cool at room temperature, then leave to pickle in the fridge for at least 24 hours.

FOR THE HAM HOCK

Preheat the oven to 110°C (230°F). Place the ham in an oven bag with the chilli oil. Transfer to a baking tray and cook in the oven for 10 hours. It is a good idea to put it in before you go to bed, then remove it in the morning.

Leave the ham until cool enough to handle, but still warm. Wearing latex gloves, remove the skin. Shred the skin into nice long pieces and discard any fat or veins. Keep the meat warm in a small saucepan if you are going to use it shortly; otherwise refrigerate until required, and gently reheat for serving.

FOR THE SICHUAN SALT & PEPPER

Toast the salt and peppercorns in a dry frying pan over medium heat until you can smell the pepper. Cool, then grind to a fine powder using a spice grinder.

TO SERVE

In a large non-stick frying pan, heat the vegetable oil over medium heat. Add the duck eggs and cook gently until the whites are almost done. Add 2 tablespoons water and put the lid on for 30 seconds to steam the top.

When the whites are done but the yolks are still runny, scatter evenly with the shredded ham and sprinkle with the sichuan salt and pepper.

Remove the okra from the pickling liquid and slice into 5 mm (¼ inch) rounds — beware, it is sticky! Arrange around the eggs, then top with the coriander cress. Serve with crusty bread.

SERVES 4 AS PART OF A SHARED MEAL

GRASS-FED PORTERHOUSE WITH CARAMELISED ONION PURÉE & PEPPER SAUCE

— 2 x 250 g (9 oz) grass-fed porterhouse steaks
— 30 ml (1 fl oz) olive oil

ONION PURÉE

— 100 g (3½ oz) butter
— 3 large brown onions, sliced
— 50 ml (1¾ fl oz) sherry vinegar

PEPPER SAUCE

— 1 tablespoon olive oil
— 100 g (3½ oz) beef trimmings
— 1 tablespoon black peppercorns, cracked
— 1 tablespoon white peppercorns, cracked
— 4 French shallots, sliced
— 2 garlic cloves, sliced
— 2 tablespoons redcurrant jelly
— 100 ml (3½ fl oz) red wine vinegar
— 2 teaspoons port
— 300 ml (10 fl oz) red wine
— 1 litre (34 fl oz/4 cups) veal stock

I love a good bit of chargrilled beef. I prefer to use grass-fed beef over grain-fed as it is better for the cattle, the environment and has better flavour. Beef and black pepper is a hard combination to top. This sauce recipe is inspired by one from the amazing Michel Roux Jr.

FOR THE ONION PURÉE

Heat the butter in a wide-based saucepan over medium heat. Add the onion and a generous sprinkle of sea salt and freshly ground black pepper. Turn the heat down to low. Cook, stirring frequently, for about 1 hour, until the onion is very soft, sweet and golden. Remove from the stove and leave to cool, then place in a blender with the vinegar and blitz to a smooth purée. Check the seasoning and set aside somewhere warm.

FOR THE PEPPER SAUCE

Heat a heavy-based saucepan over high heat and add the olive oil. Cook the beef trimmings and peppercorns until the beef is quite brown and caramelised and the juices have caramelised on the bottom. Add the shallot and garlic and sweat for about 7 minutes, until they have caramelised.

Stir in the redcurrant jelly until dissolved. Add the vinegar and reduce until almost dry. Add the port, then cook until almost dry. Now stir in the wine and cook until it has reduced by half. Add the stock and cook over low heat, skimming frequently, for about 10 minutes, until it has reduced by half.

Strain the sauce through a fine strainer and reserve in a small saucepan.

FOR THE STEAKS

Heat a barbecue or cast-iron grill plate to high. Rub the steaks with the olive oil, then cook for 5 minutes on each side, or until medium–rare. Remove from the heat, cover and leave to rest for at least 10 minutes.

TO SERVE

Quickly reheat the steaks for 1 minute on each side on the grill. Spread the onion purée along the middle of a platter. Slice each steak slightly on the bias and lay slightly spread over the purée. Generously drizzle the pepper sauce over and around the steak.

Delicious served with Slow-roasted crushed potatoes and garlic (see page 124), and plenty of crusty sourdough for mopping up the sauce!

SERVES 4 AS PART OF A SHARED MEAL

SERVE WITH CRUSTY
SOURDOUGH TO
MOP UP THE SAUCE

WAGYU & GREEN PEPPERCORN CURRY WITH COCONUT, SHALLOT & LIME LEAF

— 400 ml (13½ fl oz) coconut
milk
— lemongrass trimmings (from
making the Spice paste below)
— 4 lime leaves
— 1 tablespoon fish sauce,
plus extra to taste
— 800 g (1 lb 12 oz) wagyu
intercostals or oyster blade,
cut into 3 cm (1¼ inch) cubes
— 2 tablespoons chopped
palm sugar (jaggery)
— 100 g (3½ oz) fresh green
peppercorns
— 100 ml (3½ fl oz) coconut
cream

PICKLED SHALLOTS

— 125 ml (4 fl oz/½ cup) coconut
vinegar (see Note)
— 55 g (2 oz/¼ cup) sugar
— 4 red Asian shallots, sliced

SPICE PASTE

— 5 dried red chillies, stems
removed, soaked in hot water
— 1½ lemongrass stems, white
part only, very finely sliced
— zest of 1 kaffir lime (makrut)
— 8 coriander (cilantro) roots,
washed well
— 1 teaspoon coriander seeds,
toasted and ground
— 1 teaspoon cumin seeds,
toasted and ground

SALAD

— 80 g (2¾ oz/1 cup) shaved
coconut, toasted
— 1 handful coriander (cilantro)
— 2 red bird's eye chillies, halved,
seeded and cut into half-rounds
— 4 kaffir lime (makrut) leaves,
very finely sliced

This curry is inspired by the pork and green peppercorn dish from Australian chef David Thompson, a master of Thai cuisine. The salad plays an important role in cutting through the curry's unctuous richness.

FOR THE PICKLED SHALLOTS

Heat the vinegar and sugar, then pour over the shallots in a bowl. Cover with plastic wrap and set aside to cool. The shallots can be pickled for up to 1 week.

TO BRAISE THE BEEF

Place the coconut milk in a saucepan with the lemongrass trimmings, lime leaves, fish sauce, 200 ml (7 fl oz) water and a large pinch of sea salt. Add the beef. Bring to the boil, then reduce the heat to low and simmer for about 2 hours, or until the beef is tender, stirring occasionally.

Remove the beef from the poaching liquid and leave to cool on a tray at room temperature. Reserve the poaching liquid.

FOR THE SPICE PASTE

Place all the ingredients in a blender and blitz to a smooth paste; if needed, you can add a little of the chilli soaking water to facilitate blending. Set aside.

FOR THE CURRY

Skim 150 ml (5 fl oz) of oil off the top of the reserved braising liquid and heat it in a heavy-based saucepan. Add the spice paste and cook out over medium heat for 10–15 minutes, or until the paste is no longer raw. Add the palm sugar and cook for another 5 minutes.

Stir in the reserved braising liquid and green peppercorns and cook for 30 minutes. Now add the beef to the curry and cook for 5–10 minutes to heat through. Season with extra fish sauce to taste.

TO SERVE

Place the hot curry in a large wide bowl. Toss the salad ingredients together with the pickled shallots, using the shallot pickling liquid as a dressing. Drizzle the curry with the coconut cream, then top with the salad.

Enjoy with steamed jasmine rice and beer.

SERVES 4 AS PART OF A SHARED MEAL

COCONUT VINEGAR
IS MADE FROM
FERMENTED COCONUT
WATER AND IS USED
IN SOUTH-EAST ASIAN
CUISINES.

PORK SCHNITZEL WITH SESAME, PLUM TONKATSU, YUZU MUSTARD & DASHI MUSHROOMS

— 500 g (1 lb 2 oz) pork loin
— 2 eggs
— 100 ml (3½ fl oz) milk
— 2 tablespoons white sesame seeds, toasted
— 2 tablespoons black sesame seeds, toasted
— 200 g (7 oz) panko (Japanese breadcrumbs; see Note)
— plain (all-purpose) flour, for dusting
— vegetable oil, for pan-frying
— Plum tonkatsu (page 182), to serve

YUZU MUSTARD

— 3 tablespoons Japanese mustard
— 1 teaspoon yuzu juice (see Note on page 47)

DASHI MUSHROOMS

— 150 g (5½ oz) enoki mushrooms, trimmed
— 150 g (5½ oz) shimeji mushrooms, trimmed
— 150 g (5½ oz) shiitake mushrooms, stems removed, caps thinly sliced
— 100 ml (3½ fl oz) Dashi stock (see Basics)
— 1 teaspoon cornflour (cornstarch), mixed to a smooth paste with 1 tablespoon water
— 1 teaspoon black sesame seeds, toasted
— 1 teaspoon white sesame seeds, toasted
— 1 tablespoon sesame oil

I love Japanese tonkatsu — in fact I love just about anything that is crumbed and fried. The sweet and sour of the plum sauce is very moreish, and then the spicy mustard brings you back down to earth.

FOR THE SCHNITZELS

Cut the pork into four 125 g (4½ oz) pieces. One by one, place each slice of pork between two sheets of plastic wrap, then beat with a meat mallet or small saucepan until about 3 mm (⅛ inch) thick.

Whisk together the eggs and milk. Toss the sesame seeds through the panko and season the mixture with sea salt and freshly ground black pepper.

Season each pork portion with salt and pepper. Dust with the flour, then dip into the egg wash, then into the crumbs. Press the crumbs on firmly.

Repeat the egg wash and crumbing procedure for each schnitzel. Place in the fridge for 30 minutes to allow the crumbs to set.

FOR THE YUZU MUSTARD

Mix the ingredients together and set aside.

FOR THE MUSHROOMS

Bring the mushrooms and stock to the boil in a saucepan. Stir in the cornflour paste, stirring to thicken. Simmer for 5 minutes, until the cornflour taste has cooked out; if the sauce is too thick, add a little more stock. Remove from the heat and stir the sesame seeds and oil through. Reserve at room temperature.

TO SERVE

Heat 1 cm (½ inch) of oil in a large frying pan over medium heat.
Cook the schnitzels for 3–5 minutes on each side, or until golden and crisp. Remove from the pan and drain on paper towel. Season with sea salt.

Cut each schnitzel into three pieces and arrange on a platter. Drizzle the plum tonkatsu sauce over the slices. Put small dots of mushrooms around and serve the yuzu mustard on the side.

SERVES 4 AS PART OF A SHARED MEAL

LAND

A JAPANESE INGREDIENT, PANKO BREADCRUMBS ARE MADE WITHOUT THE CRUST OF THE BREAD, AND ARE COARSER AND CRUNCHIER THAN REGULAR BREADCRUMBS.

CHARGRILLED QUAIL WITH PROSCIUTTO & PEACH & WITLOF SALAD

- — 4 quails
- — 1 garlic clove, crushed
- — 100 ml (3½ fl oz) olive oil
- — 4 slices prosciutto

PEACH & WITLOF SALAD

- — 4 ripe peaches
- — 125 ml (4 fl oz/½ cup) extra virgin olive oil, plus extra for drizzling
- — 25 ml (¾ fl oz) hazelnut oil
- — 50 ml (1¾ fl oz) red wine vinegar
- — 2 white witlof (chicory/endive), trimmed and separated
- — 2 red witlof (chicory/endive), trimmed and separated
- — 35 g (1¼ oz/¼ cup) roasted hazelnuts (see Note), peeled and roughly chopped

This is pretty much a match made in heaven. It is outrageously simple, but the flavours explode in your mouth. The trick is excellent prosciutto (sorry but the Italians do it best), ripe peaches, perfectly roasted hazelnuts, and smoky just-cooked grilled quail ...

TO FLATBONE POULTRY

Make a cut along the back of the quail, then lift the skin on one side. Using the tip of a small knife, start to remove the flesh from along the shoulder blade, then cut through the shoulder socket to release the wing. Pull the leg bone away from the body to pop it out of the joint, then use the knife to remove the flesh. To remove the breast, look for a line of fat along the edge of the breast where it joins the rib cage. Keeping the tip of your knife on the rib cage, gently cut the breast away, then repeat the process on the other side. Now remove the whole breast from the bone by gently slicing it along that bone, without cutting through the skin. Finally remove the thigh bones by cutting along the bone to release it, then cut through the joint to remove the bone.

•
TO ROAST HAZELNUTS, BAKE THEM IN A 160°C (320°F) OVEN FOR 7–10 MINUTES, OR UNTIL AROMATIC, TOSSING EVERY FEW MINUTES SO THEY DON'T BURN. RUB WITH A CLOTH TO REMOVE THE PAPERY SKINS.

FOR THE QUAIL

Mix the garlic with the olive oil, then spread evenly over each quail. Cover and marinate in the fridge for 2 hours.

Heat a barbecue or cast-iron grill plate to high. Grill the quails, skin side down, for 3 minutes, then turn over and cook the other side for 2 minutes. Remove from the heat, cover and leave to rest.

FOR THE SALAD

Cut the peaches in half. Remove the stones, then slice each peach half into four wedges and place in a mixing bowl. Put the olive oil, hazelnut oil and vinegar in a bottle with a little sea salt and freshly ground black pepper and shake well.

Gently toss the peach with the witlof leaves and hazelnuts. Dress lightly with the vinaigrette, then season and arrange on a large platter.

TO SERVE

Tear each prosciutto slice in half lengthways and drape over the salad. Cut each quail in half and arrange around the salad. Drizzle with a little extra olive oil and serve.

SERVES 4 AS PART OF A SHARED MEAL

THE TRICK
IS EXCELLENT
PROSCIUTTO!

RED WINE BRAISED BEEF SHORT RIBS WITH PARSNIP PURÉE & PERSILLADE

- — 1 kg (2 lb 3 oz) beef short ribs, trimmed of sinew
- — plain (all-purpose) flour, for dusting, plus an extra 25 g (1 oz/scant ¼ cup) to thicken the sauce
- — 100 ml (3½ fl oz) olive oil
- — 1 onion, roughly diced
- — 1 carrot, chopped
- — 2 celery stalks, chopped
- — 1 leek, white part only, sliced
- — 8 thyme sprigs
- — 10 whole garlic cloves, peeled
- — 2 bay leaves
- — 1 x 750 ml (25½ fl oz) bottle red wine
- — 25 g (1 oz) butter

CONTINUES OPPOSITE →

This dish is a real mid-winter rib-sticker. It screams comfort food and just makes you feel happy inside. It is pretty easy to pull off too. Make sure you get decent-sized short ribs from your butcher, and obviously cook it on the bone.

FOR THE RIBS

Preheat the oven to 175°C (345°F) — or 100°C (210°F) if you have time to slowly cook the ribs overnight.

Season the ribs with sea salt and freshly ground black pepper, then dust with flour, shaking off the excess.

Heat a large non-stick frying pan over medium heat and add a little olive oil. Cook the ribs on all sides until they're nicely browned and a lovely crust has formed. Place the ribs in a flameproof casserole dish that will fit them all snugly with all the vegetables and the wine.

Heat the remaining olive oil in the frying pan. Add the onion, carrot, celery, leek, thyme and garlic cloves and sauté for 10 minutes, until the vegetables start to caramelise.

Add the sautéed vegetables to the ribs, poking them into the gaps. Add the bay leaves and wine, and a little water if needed to bring the liquid up to the top of the ribs. Bring to the boil.

Cover the dish with a sheet of baking paper, then foil. Transfer to the oven and cook for 3 hours at the higher temperature, or overnight at the lower temperature, until the ribs are very tender. Let the ribs cool in the liquid.

Remove the ribs from the braising liquid. Strain the liquid through a fine sieve into a saucepan and reduce over low heat for 20–30 minutes, skimming frequently. Meanwhile, slide the bones away from the ribs and place the meat into the fridge to set. Once cold, trim the gelatinous part from where the rib hangs onto the bone, then square the ribs up so they are neat.

Once the sauce tastes balanced, mix the butter and the extra 25 g (1 oz) flour together in a bowl with your hands until the mixture resembles coarse sand. Whisk into the sauce to thicken it, then simmer for 10 minutes, until the flour taste is cooked out.

When almost ready to serve, return the ribs to the sauce for 10 minutes to warm through.

Continues opposite →

**CONTINUED FROM
PREVIOUS PAGE →**

PARSNIP PURÉE

— 1 kg (2 lb 3 oz) parsnip,
  peeled, ends removed, sliced
  into rounds
— 500 ml (17 fl oz/2 cups) milk
— 100 g (3½ oz) butter
— 100 ml (3½ fl oz) thin
  (pouring) cream
— ground white pepper, to taste

PERSILLADE

— 1 large handful picked flat-leaf
  (Italian) parsley
— 4 garlic cloves
— 100 ml (3½ fl oz) extra virgin
  olive oil

FOR THE PARSNIP PURÉE

Place the parsnip in a saucepan with the milk. Cover the mixture with a round of baking paper and cook over low heat for 45 minutes, or until the parsnip is fully cooked. (Don't be tempted to cook the mixture over a higher heat, or the milk will scorch on the bottom of the pan.)

Strain and discard the milk, then drain the parsnip well and place in a blender. Add the butter and cream, season with sea salt and ground white pepper and whiz to a very smooth purée — it should taste delicious!

Pass through a fine strainer, into a clean saucepan. Cover the purée with a lid to keep warm.

FOR THE PERSILLADE

Finely chop the parsley with the garlic. Place in a mixing bowl and mix the olive oil through. Season to taste with salt and pepper.

TO SERVE

Spoon the parsnip purée onto the bottom of a platter, if sharing, or four large wide bowls, leaving a bit of a crater in the middle. Arrange the ribs in the centre, then spoon the sauce over the ribs. Drizzle with the persillade.

Delicious served with Roasted brussels sprouts and portobello mushrooms (see page 132) — and of course a big, gutsy red wine!

SERVES 4 AS PART OF A SHARED MEAL

SALT & PEPPER

PERSILLADE

PARSNIP
PURÉE

RED WINE BRAISED
BEEF SHORT RIBS

SMOKED PORK CHEEK WITH COCONUT SAUCE, FINGER LIME & LYCHEES

- 100 ml (3½ fl oz) fish sauce
- 50 g (1¾ oz/¼ cup) chopped palm sugar (jaggery)
- 2 large pig's cheeks, skinned and trimmed, cut into slices 5 mm (¼ inch) thick
- wood chips, for smoking
- 30 g (1 oz/½ cup) flaked coconut, toasted
- 6 lychees, peeled, stoned and quartered
- 1 finger lime (see Note), podded
- 3 tablespoons picked Thai basil
- thinly shredded kaffir lime (makrut) leaves, to garnish
- snipped coriander (cilantro) cress, to garnish

COCONUT SAUCE (TOM KHA)

- 200 ml (7 fl oz) coconut milk
- 3 thin slices fresh galangal, about 2 cm (¾ inch) round
- 1 whole lemongrass stalk, bruised and chopped
- 1 garlic clove
- 1 red Asian shallot, sliced
- 1 tablespoon palm sugar (jaggery)
- juice of ½ lime

I came up with this dish when asked to help prepare a welcome dinner for international guests for the 2012 Melbourne Food and Wine Festival. It sums up some of the flavours and techniques I love.

In a saucepan, heat the fish sauce, palm sugar and 300 ml (10 fl oz) water until the sugar has dissolved. Leave to cool, then pour into a container large enough to hold the pig's cheeks. Add the pig's cheeks to the liquid, then cover and refrigerate for 6 hours.

Heat the wood chips in a smoker or kettle barbecue until they start to smoke. Remove the cheeks from the brine and pat dry. Place on a rack in the smoker or barbecue. Reduce the heat to low, cover and leave to smoke for 2 hours.

Towards the end of smoking time, preheat the oven to 110°C (230°F).

Place the smoked cheeks on a baking tray, then transfer to the oven and bake for 6–8 hours, until very soft. Remove and cool in the fridge.

FOR THE COCONUT SAUCE

Combine all the ingredients in a saucepan with 50 ml (1¾ fl oz) water. Cook over medium heat for 20–30 minutes, until the sauce is just thick and all the flavours have come together. Strain and cool.

TO SERVE

Fry the pig's cheeks in a non-stick frying pan over medium heat until just lightly crisp and warmed through.

Warm the coconut sauce and place on the bottom of a plate. Top with the pig's cheeks.

Mix the coconut, lychee and lime in a mixing bowl. Tear in the Thai basil, toss together, then sprinkle over the dish. Serve garnished with the shredded lime leaves and coriander cress.

SERVES 4 AS PART OF A SHARED MEAL

FINGER LIME IS AN AUSTRALIAN NATIVE FRUIT. THE SIZE OF A THUMB, IT IS FILLED WITH CAVIAR-LIKE SEGMENTS OF INTENSELY FRAGRANT LIME FLAVOUR THAT POP IN YOUR MOUTH.

THIS IS AN INCREDIBLY
RICH AND INTENSELY
FLAVOURED DISH,
BUT I THINK IT IS VERY
WELL BALANCED

RARE SESAME BEEF SALAD WITH LEMONGRASS, LIME, PEANUTS & RICE PADDY HERB

— 1 x 500 g (1 lb 2 oz) grass-fed beef eye fillet, trimmed of sinew
— 25 ml (¾ fl oz) fish sauce
— 1 lemongrass stem, white part only, finely chopped
— 1 tablespoon peanut oil
— 1 handful picked mint, torn
— 1 handful picked rice paddy herb
— 2 red Asian shallots, sliced
— 40 g (1½ oz/¼ cup) roasted and coarsely chopped peanuts
— snipped coriander (cilantro) cress, to garnish

LEMONGRASS & LIME DRESSING

— 1 lemongrass stem, white part only, finely chopped
— 1 garlic clove, peeled
— 1 red Asian shallot
— 1 red bird's eye chilli, sliced
— 25 ml (¾ fl oz) fish sauce
— 2 tablespoons chopped palm sugar (jaggery)
— 50 ml (1¾ fl oz) lime juice

VERMICELLI

— vegetable oil, for deep-frying
— 20 g (¾ oz/½ cup) dry bean thread vermicelli noodles
— ½ teaspoon chilli powder

This salad was inspired by my first trip to Hoi An in Vietnam. It is light and refreshing, but has lots of flavour going on. The rice paddy herb can be found at good Vietnamese grocers and has a flavour not unlike a lemony cumin. You can prepare the beef, dressing and salad ingredients in advance, and whip it up at the last minute.

Preheat the oven to 160°C (320°F).

Rub the beef with the fish sauce and lemongrass. Heat a large non-stick frying pan over high heat and add the oil. Cook the beef for about 20 seconds on each side, then place on a baking tray and roast for 5 minutes.

Remove from the oven and leave to rest for 15 minutes. Wrap tightly in plastic wrap and place in the fridge to chill.

FOR THE LEMONGRASS & LIME DRESSING

Blitz all the ingredients in a blender until smooth. Set aside.

FOR THE VERMICELLI

Heat about 5 cm (2 inches) of vegetable oil in a large saucepan to 180°C (355°F). Test by dipping a wooden chopstick into the oil: the chopstick will sizzle when the oil is ready. Add the noodles and briefly cook until crisp and puffed — they will puff up very quickly. Remove and drain well on paper towel. Toss with the chilli powder and set aside.

TO SERVE

Using a sharp knife, and leaving the beef in the plastic wrap to keep its shape, slice the chilled beef as thinly as possible and remove all the plastic wrap. Toss the beef in a large bowl with the herbs, shallot, peanuts and dressing.

Spread the salad on a platter. Top with the vermicelli noodles and coriander cress and serve.

SERVES 4 AS PART OF A SHARED MEAL

FIVE-SPICE CRISPY QUAIL WITH GREEN MANGO SALAD, RADISH & CASHEWS

- 4 quails, halved, breast bone removed
- vegetable oil, for deep-frying
- plain (all-purpose) flour, for dusting
- snipped coriander (cilantro) cress, to garnish

MARINADE

- 3 tablespoons sea salt
- 3 tablespoons sugar
- 2 tablespoons sichuan peppercorns, ground
- 1 tablespoon Chinese five-spice
- 190 ml (6½ fl oz/¾ cup) light soy sauce
- 190 ml (6½ fl oz/¾ cup) shaoxing rice wine
- 2 cm (¾ inch) knob fresh ginger, peeled and finely grated
- 1 garlic clove, crushed

PALM SUGAR & CHILLI DRESSING

- 100 g (3½ oz) palm sugar (jaggery), chopped
- 125 ml (4 fl oz/½ cup) fish sauce
- 30 ml (1 fl oz) coconut vinegar (see Note, page 92)
- 50 ml (1¾ fl oz) lime juice
- 1 garlic clove, crushed
- 1 long red chilli, seeded and finely diced

GREEN MANGO SALAD

- 2 green mangoes
- 4 radishes, finely sliced
- 155 g (5½ oz/1 cup) roasted cashew nuts
- 1½ tablespoons finely sliced saw-tooth coriander (cilantro)

Quail is a delicious morsel to enjoy when you want to get your hands dirty. When green mango is in season I can't get enough of it — I love the tanginess and crunch it adds to dishes.

TO MARINATE THE QUAIL

Mix all the marinade ingredients together in a container large enough to hold all the quail. Add the quail halves and toss to coat. Cover and marinate in the fridge for 6 hours.

FOR THE PALM SUGAR & CHILLI DRESSING

In a saucepan over medium heat, melt the palm sugar in 100 ml (3½ fl oz) water until dissolved. Leave to cool, then stir in the remaining ingredients.

FOR THE GREEN MANGO SALAD

Peel the skin off the mangoes. Using a vegetable peeler, cut the flesh into thin strips. Lay the mango strips on a chopping board and slice them into ribbons 1 cm (½ inch) wide. Place in a bowl with the remaining salad ingredients.

TO SERVE

Heat about 10 cm (4 inches) of vegetable oil in a large saucepan to 180°C (355°F). Test by dipping a wooden chopstick into the oil: the chopstick will sizzle when the oil is ready.

Remove the quail from the marinade and pat dry with paper towel. Dust the quails in the flour, shaking off the excess. Working in two batches, gently drop the quail into the hot oil and cook for 4–5 minutes, until golden and crispy. Remove with a slotted spoon and drain immediately on paper towel.

While still hot, toss the quail in a large mixing bowl with all the salad ingredients and the dressing.

Arrange the salad and quail on a platter and top with coriander cress.

SERVES 4 AS PART OF A SHARED MEAL

ROASTED DUCK BREAST WITH PICKLED CHERRIES, HAZELNUT QUINOA & HERBED GOAT'S CURD

- 2 x 250 g (9 oz) duck breasts, trimmed of sinew and excess fat
- snipped coriander (cilantro) cress, to garnish

PICKLED CHERRIES

- 250 g (9 oz) cherries, pitted and halved
- 100 ml (3½ fl oz) red wine vinegar

HAZELNUT QUINOA

- 200 g (7 oz/1 cup) quinoa, prepared as directed on page 117
- 100 ml (3½ fl oz) extra virgin olive oil
- 55 g (2 oz/⅓ cup) roasted and halved hazelnuts

HERBED GOAT'S CURD

- 200 g (7 oz) goat's curd
- 2 thyme sprigs, picked and chopped

FOR THE PICKLED CHERRIES

In a container, mix the cherries with the vinegar. Season with freshly ground black pepper and place in the fridge for at least 24 hours before using.

FOR THE HAZELNUT QUINOA

Place the cooked quinoa in a large bowl. Stir in the olive oil and season to taste.

Preheat the oven to 160°C (320°F). Evenly spread the quinoa over a baking tray and roast for 45 minutes, or until it is all crisp. Make sure you mix it around every 10 minutes or so, as the edges will toast faster than the middle.

Cool, transfer to a bowl and toss the hazelnuts through.

TO COOK THE DUCK

Increase the oven temperature to 180°C (355°F). Season the duck with sea salt and black pepper and rub in well. Using a sharp knife, score the skin in a crisscross pattern.

Cook the duck in an ovenproof frying pan, skin side down, over medium heat for about 5 minutes, until the skin is crisp and golden. Turn the duck over, then transfer the pan to the oven and roast for 4 minutes.

Turn the duck over again and roast for a further 2 minutes. The duck should be somewhere in between medium–rare and medium — rosy but not raw. Place the duck on a rack and leave to rest for at least 10 minutes.

FOR THE HERBED GOAT'S CURD

Combine the ingredients in a bowl and season with salt and pepper. Whip with a whisk and set aside.

TO SERVE

Pile the quinoa mixture on a platter. Arrange the pickled cherries around. Smear the goat's curd along one side.

Flash the duck breasts in the oven for 5 minutes, then cut on the bias into slices 5 mm (¼ inch) thick, starting at the pointy end. Arrange the duck slices over the quinoa. Sprinkle the duck with a little salt and garnish with the coriander cress.

SERVES 4 AS PART OF A SHARED MEAL

SERVE WITH A SMEAR
OF GOAT'S CURD

 LAND

WAGYU BEEF TATAKI WITH ROASTED SHALLOT & CHILLI DRESSING & TOASTED RICE

— 1 x 300 g (10½ oz) wagyu eye fillet, preferably centre cut
— 50 ml (1¾ fl oz) fish sauce
— snipped mustard cress, to garnish

ROASTED SHALLOT & CHILLI DRESSING

— 2 large red Asian shallots, unpeeled
— 2 red bird's eye chillies, stems removed
— 1 tablespoon vegetable oil
— 2 dried red chillies
— 50 ml (1¾ fl oz) fish sauce
— 50 ml (1¾ fl oz) lime juice
— 1 garlic clove
— 1 teaspoon chopped palm sugar (jaggery)

TOASTED RICE

— 50 g (1¾ oz/¼ cup) jasmine rice
— 1 teaspoon coriander seeds
— 1 small dried red chilli, broken into a few pieces

FRIED SHALLOTS

— vegetable oil, for deep-frying
— 2 red Asian shallots, finely sliced

I love raw beef just as much as cooked beef. Eye fillet is perfect for tataki, due to the subtle flavour of that cut. The dressing is intense in flavour and the ground rice adds nice crunch for texture.

Rub the beef with the fish sauce. Heat a non-stick frying pan over high heat, then sear the beef for about 15 seconds on each side, so it has a browned exterior but is not really cooked at all. Leave to cool, then wrap tightly with plastic wrap and leave to chill in the fridge for at least 3 hours.

FOR THE ROASTED SHALLOT & CHILLI DRESSING

Preheat the oven to 175°C (345°F). Rub the unpeeled shallots and bird's eye chillies with the oil and wrap in foil. Roast for 20–30 minutes, until soft. You may need to pull the chillies out first so they don't burn. The shallots need to be completely soft.

Meanwhile, roast the dried chillies in the oven for 4–5 minutes, until crisp and lightly coloured, but not burnt.

Allow the roasted shallots and bird's eye chillies to cool a little. Cut the tips off and squeeze the insides into a blender. Add the dried chillies and remaining dressing ingredients and blitz until a smooth dressing has formed. Set aside.

FOR THE TOASTED RICE

Fry the rice, coriander seeds and chilli pieces in a dry non-stick frying pan over low heat, stirring frequently, until the rice becomes opaque. Using a spice grinder, blitz the mixture to the consistency of coarse sand. Set aside.

FOR THE FRIED SHALLOTS

Heat 5 cm (2 inches) of oil in a medium-sized saucepan to 180°C (355°F). Fry the shallots until golden. Drain on paper towel and season with sea salt.

TO SERVE

Using a sharp knife, and leaving the beef in the plastic wrap to keep its shape, cut the chilled beef into slices about 3 mm (⅛ inch) thick. Remove the plastic and leave to sit for 10 minutes until the beef comes to room temperature.

Spread a generous circle of the dressing on a large plate. Arrange the beef on top. Serve sprinkled with the toasted rice, fried shallots and mustard cress.

SERVES 4 AS PART OF A SHARED MEAL

LAND

EARTH

BABY CARROTS WITH ZUCCHINI, GOAT'S CURD, POMEGRANATE & TARRAGON DRESSING

— 500 g (1 lb 2 oz) striped zucchini (courgettes)
— 100 ml (3½ fl oz) chardonnay vinegar
— 500 g (1 lb 2 oz) mixed baby heirloom carrots, topped and washed
— 1 pomegranate
— 200 g (7 oz) goat's curd
— snipped red sorrel cress, to garnish

TARRAGON DRESSING

— 100 ml (3½ fl oz) chardonnay vinegar
— 200 ml (7 fl oz) extra virgin olive oil
— 10 French tarragon sprigs, picked
— 1 tablespoon dijon mustard
— pinch of citric acid

The freshness of this salad has made it a popular summer dish at Huxtable. We use produce from a wonderful organic farmer called Andrew Wood. His striped zucchini, heirloom carrots and French tarragon really were the stars of this dish.

FOR THE TARRAGON DRESSING

Combine all the ingredients in a blender and blitz until combined. Store in a clean glass jar until needed; the dressing keeps well for several days.

FOR THE ZUCCHINI

Wash the zucchini and cut off the ends. Using a mandoline or vegetable peeler, cut the zucchini into long ribbons. Scatter the ribbons over a large tray and sprinkle with the vinegar and some sea salt and freshly ground black pepper. Leave to sit for 30 minutes to lightly pickle and macerate.

FOR THE CARROTS

Bring a saucepan of salted water to the boil. Cut the carrots in half if they are large, otherwise leave them whole. Place them in the boiling water and cook for 4–5 minutes, or until just done — you still want them to be firm. Remove and chill in iced water. When the carrots are cold, remove and drain on paper towel.

TO SEED THE POMEGRANATE

Sit the pomegranate on an old chopping board, with the 'crown' facing up. (The juice stains boards and fingers, so you may like to wear latex gloves.) Using a sharp knife, cut down halfway through the fruit, then gently pull it apart with your hands. Now cut down halfway through each pomegranate half again, then gently pull each half into quarters. Using your fingers, very gently prise the seeds from the membranes of each section, trying not to break the juicy flesh of the seeds. Discard the membranes and peel, and set the seeds aside.

TO SERVE

In a large bowl, toss the zucchini with the carrots and a decent amount of the dressing to coat. Season, then arrange nicely on a platter.

Use a disposable piping (icing) bag to make small dots of goat's curd, the size of marbles, around the salad. Scatter the salad with the pomegranate seeds, then whimsically scatter the red sorrel cress all over and serve.

SERVES 4 AS PART OF A SHARED MEAL

SALAD OF ASPARAGUS, BROCCOLINI, BEANS & SESAME GINGER DRESSING

— 400 g (14 oz) broccolini
— 10–12 asparagus spears
— 500 g (1 lb 2 oz) green beans, as small as possible

SESAME GINGER DRESSING

— 80 g (2¾ oz/½ cup) sesame seeds, toasted
— 40 g (1½ oz/¼ cup) peanuts, roasted
— 1 tablespoon soy sauce
— 1 tablespoon mirin
— 1 teaspoon sugar
— 1 teaspoon finely grated fresh ginger

This is a pimped-up version of the Japanese sesame spinach I love, served with the Dashi-poached eggs on page 50. I love my greens and this dish contains three of my favourites. The greens can be blanched and refreshed and kept in the fridge ahead of time, then dressed at the last minute.

FOR THE SESAME GINGER DRESSING

Blitz all the ingredients in a food processor until smooth and thick, adding a little water if necessary to thin the dressing. The dressing can be refrigerated in a clean glass jar for several days; bring to room temperature for serving.

FOR THE SALAD

Trim about 1 cm (½ inch) from the cut ends of the broccolini, then peel the long stalks using a vegetable peeler.

Trim the asparagus stems, so the spears are about 12 cm (4¾ inches) long. Test that you have cut the woody part away by slicing a small disc from the end and tasting it. Peel the spears lightly using a vegetable peeler — about 3 cm (1¼ inches) from the tip for thick spears, but don't worry about peeling thinner younger ones.

To prepare the beans, just cut the stalk end off.

Bring a large saucepan of salted water to the boil. Cook the vegetables, one type at a time, for 4–5 minutes each, then remove and refresh in iced water.

Drain the vegetables well on paper towel. Cut all the vegetables in thirds, on the diagonal.

When ready to serve, toss the vegetables with a generous amount of the dressing and present in a large bowl or on a platter.

SERVES 4 AS PART OF A SHARED MEAL

TOSS THE VEGETABLES
WITH A GENEROUS
AMOUNT OF SESAME
DRESSING

EARTH

LEBANESE CAULIFLOWER WITH HARISSA YOGHURT & PISTACHIO DUKKAH

— vegetable oil, for deep-frying
— 1 cauliflower, cut into large florets
— coriander (cilantro) cress, to garnish

HARISSA YOGHURT

— 500 g (1 lb 2 oz/2 cups) plain yoghurt
— 2 tablespoons Harissa (page 180)

PISTACHIO DUKKAH

— 140 g (5 oz/1 cup) hazelnuts
— 155 g (5½ oz/1 cup) blanched almonds
— 150 g (5½ oz/1 cup) shelled pistachio nuts
— 50 g (1¾ oz/⅓ cup) sesame seeds
— 30 g (1 oz/⅓ cup) coriander seeds
— 2 tablespoons cumin seeds
— 2 heaped tablespoons ground coriander
— 3 heaped tablespoons ground cumin
— 1 heaped tablespoon dried thyme
— 3 heaped tablespoons za'atar (see Note)

FOR THE HARISSA YOGHURT

Line a sieve with muslin (cheesecloth) and set over a bowl. Put the yoghurt in the sieve and leave to drain overnight in the fridge.

The next day, mix the harissa through the yoghurt and set aside.

FOR THE PISTACHIO DUKKAH

Preheat the oven to 160°C (320°F). Roast the hazelnuts, almonds and pistachios on separate baking trays for 5–10 minutes, or until aromatic and lightly coloured, tossing the nuts every few minutes so they don't burn. Remove from the oven and leave to cool. Place the hazelnuts in a cloth and rub off the papery skins.

Separately toast the sesame seeds, coriander seeds and cumin seeds in a dry frying pan over medium heat for a few minutes each time, until fragrant, then tip them into a bowl. Add the ground coriander and ground cumin to the pan, toast until fragrant, then add to the other toasted spices.

Put the roasted almonds and the pistachios in a food processor and pulse until fine (but not too fine, or the oil will release from the nuts). Transfer to a bowl. Finely pulse the hazelnuts and add to the almonds.

Now blitz the toasted seeds and spices in the food processor to break up the seeds. Add to the nuts with the thyme and za'atar. Season well with sea salt and freshly ground black pepper. You won't need all the dukkah for this recipe; the leftovers will keep in an airtight container for up to 1 month.

ZA'ATAR IS A MIDDLE EASTERN SPICE MIX CONTAINING SESAME SEEDS, SUMAC AND DRIED HERBS SUCH AS THYME. IT IS SOLD IN SPICE SHOPS.

TO DEEP-FRY THE CAULIFLOWER

Heat about 5 cm (2 inches) of vegetable oil in a large saucepan to 180°C (355°F). Test by dipping a wooden chopstick into the oil: the chopstick will sizzle if the oil is ready. Working in two batches, gently lower the cauliflower into the hot oil and cook for 3–5 minutes, until chestnut brown. Remove using a slotted spoon and drain on paper towel. Season with sea salt.

TO SERVE

Smear the harissa yoghurt over a large plate or platter. Arrange the cauliflower on top, with the florets facing up. Sprinkle liberally with dukkah, scatter with coriander cress and serve.

SERVES 4 AS PART OF A SHARED MEAL

MASALA OKRA & MORNING GLORY

- 100 ml (3½ fl oz) olive oil
- 500 g (1 lb 2 oz) okra,
  stalks removed, pods sliced
  diagonally 1 cm (½ inch) thick
- 250 g (9 oz) morning glory
  (see Note), tough stalks
  removed, leaves chopped into
  5 cm (2 inch) lengths, washed
  well and dried

MASALA PASTE

- 100 ml (3½ fl oz) olive oil
- 2 garlic cloves, crushed
- 2 red Asian shallots, finely
  chopped
- 2 cm (¾ inch) knob
  fresh ginger, peeled and
  finely chopped
- 1 lemongrass stem, white part
  only, finely chopped
- ¼ teaspoon chilli powder
- ¼ teaspoon ground turmeric
- 1 teaspoon ground coriander
- ½ teaspoon ground cumin
- 200 ml (7 fl oz) tomato
  passata (puréed tomatoes)
- 1 teaspoon brown sugar
- 1 tablespoon lemon juice

These greens are commonly eaten in our house. My wife grew up eating them in Malaysia and we love to have them just sautéed with garlic, ginger, turmeric and chilli. However, this simple masala sauce is quick to make and absolutely delicious.

FOR THE MASALA PASTE

Heat the olive oil in a wide-based saucepan over medium heat. Add the garlic, shallot, ginger and lemongrass and cook for 3–4 minutes, or until fragrant. Add the dry spices and cook for a further 3–4 minutes.

Add the tomato passata and sugar and simmer over low heat for 15 minutes, or until the sauce starts to thicken slightly. Add the lemon juice and season with sea salt and freshly ground black pepper. Set aside to cool.

The masala can be made up to a week ahead and refrigerated in an airtight container until required.

TO SERVE

Heat the oil over high heat in a wok or large frying pan.

Add the okra and cook for 2 minutes, or until just starting to soften. Add the morning glory and sauté for 1 minute.

Stir in the masala sauce and cook until it is heated through, and the greens are just cooked. Transfer to a bowl and serve.

SERVES 4 AS PART OF A SHARED MEAL

MORNING GLORY, ALSO
KNOWN AS WATER
SPINACH OR KANG KONG,
IS A LEAFY, STALKY GREEN
VEGETABLE WIDELY USED
IN ASIA, OFTEN STIR-FRIED
WITH GARLIC AND CHILLI.
IT IS HIGH IN CALCIUM —
GREAT FOR THOSE UNABLE
TO CONSUME DAIRY.

EARTH

QUINOA, THE SUPERFOOD
OF THE PAST DECADE!

QUINOA SALAD OF ZUCCHINI FLOWERS, POMEGRANATE & GOAT'S CHEESE

— 200 g (7 oz/1 cup) quinoa
— 8 zucchini (courgette) flowers, stamens removed, flowers halved lengthways
— 12 mint leaves, washed
— 200 g (7 oz) marinated goat's feta
— 1 pomegranate, seeded (see method on page 110)
— 100 g (3½ oz) cashew nuts, toasted
— 100 ml (3½ fl oz) extra virgin olive oil
— 30 ml (1 fl oz) lemon juice

Quinoa: the superfood of the past decade. An ancient grain that contains all nine essential amino acids, it has risen in popularity and is now found on menus everywhere. It is also gluten free, which is a bonus. I decided to do this salad with lightly blanched zucchini flowers, instead of the usual deep-fried ones.

TO PREPARE QUINOA

Bring a saucepan of salted water to the boil. Place the quinoa in a sieve and wash under cold running water until the water runs clear. Gently place the rinsed quinoa into the boiling water, stir, then simmer for 12 minutes.

Strain the quinoa in a sieve (not a colander, as the quinoa will pass straight through it). Place the sieve under running water until the quinoa is cool. Leave to drain thoroughly, then place on a tray or plate. Leave uncovered in the fridge to dry out a little; the quinoa can be cooked up to a day ahead.

FOR THE ZUCCHINI FLOWERS

Bring a separate saucepan of salted water to the boil. Add the zucchini flowers and cook for 30 seconds. Remove with a slotted spoon and place the flowers in iced water to stop them cooking. Once cold, remove from the water and drain on paper towel.

TO SERVE

Place the quinoa in a large bowl and add the mint, tearing it up with your hands. Add the rest of the ingredients, season to taste with sea salt and freshly ground black pepper and toss well to mix, being careful not to break the flowers.

Serve in a large bowl or platter, ensuring the components are all visible and nicely arranged on the top.

SERVES 4 AS PART OF A SHARED MEAL

WARM SALAD OF SWEET CORN & BLACK BEANS WITH CHIPOTLE & LIME CRÈME FRAÎCHE

— 2 cobs sweet corn,
  in their husks
— 100 g (3½ oz) dried black
  turtle beans, soaked in cold
  water overnight
— 50 g (1¾ oz) ghee
  (clarified butter)
— pinch of bicarbonate of soda
  (baking soda)
— snipped basil cress, to garnish

CHIPOTLE & LIME CRÈME FRAÎCHE

— 150 g (5½ oz) crème fraîche
— 1 tablespoon puréed and
  strained chipotle chillies
  in adobo sauce (see Note)
— 1 tablespoon lime juice

With its South-Western US style, this is one of Huxtable's most loved dishes. The sweetness of the corn with the spicy, zesty crème fraîche is a winner.

FOR THE CORN

Heat the oven to 175°C (345°F). Place the whole cobs on a baking tray and bake for 40 minutes, turning every 10 minutes so all four sides have had a turn. Remove from the oven and leave until to cool enough to handle.

Peel the husks off the corn and trim the ends. Cut each cob in half, into two smaller cobs, to make them easier to handle. I know you will want to stand the corn on its end and cut down, but resist the urge! With the corn on its side, place your knife in one of the lines in between two rows of kernels, then slowly cut around the cob that way. By doing this you end up with all perfect kernels — not those unsightly little pieces that cutting straight down produces.

FOR THE BEANS

Drain the soaked beans and place in a saucepan. Cover with plenty of water, and add the bicarbonate of soda and a pinch of sea salt. Bring to a simmer and skim off the froth, then simmer for 30 minutes, or until the beans are tender, but still hold their shape. Drain in a colander and cool on a tray.

FOR THE CHIPOTLE & LIME CRÈME FRAÎCHE

Place the crème fraîche in a cold bowl with the chipotle purée and lime juice. Using a hand whisk, beat until thick. Cover and set aside in the fridge.

•
CHIPOTLE ARE SMOKE-DRIED RIPE JALAPEÑO CHILLIES. YOU CAN FIND THEM COOKED IN A RICH, SMOKY, SPICY SAUCE CALLED ADOBO, SOLD IN TINS AT GOOD SOUTH AMERICAN FOOD STORES.

TO SERVE

Heat the ghee in a large non-stick frying pan over high heat. Add the corn; be careful as sometimes the kernels like to explode! Cook for 2 minutes, until the corn is just starting to colour a little, then add the beans and cook for another 1–2 minutes. Season well with sea salt and freshly ground black pepper.

Spoon the corn and beans into a dish at least 2 cm (¾ inch) deep. Pipe or spoon several dollops of the crème fraîche around the top, then scatter with basil cress. Serve immediately, before the crème fraîche melts.

SERVES 4 AS PART OF A SHARED MEAL

SWEET CORN & MACARONI CHEESE WITH SMOKED MOZZARELLA & CHIPOTLE

— 2 cobs sweet corn,
  in their husks
— 250 g (9 oz) macaroni
— 50 g (1¾ oz) ghee
  (clarified butter)
— 3 tablespoons finely
  sliced chives
— 200 g (7 oz) scamorza
  (smoked mozzarella), cut into
  1 cm (½ inch) cubes

CHIPOTLE SAUCE

— 25 g (1 oz) butter
— 25 g (1 oz/scant ¼ cup) plain
  (all-purpose) flour
— 500 ml (17 fl oz/2 cups) milk
— 100 g (3½ oz) cheddar, grated
— 1 tablespoon puréed and
  strained chipotle chillies
  in adobo sauce (see Note,
  opposite)

This dish is great for winter and proving to be a crowd favourite. The key is to stir in the diced smoked mozzarella just before serving, so when people spoon out a serve it is stringy and stretchy.

FOR THE CORN

Heat the oven to 175°C (345°F). Place the whole cobs on a baking tray and bake for 40 minutes, turning every 10 minutes so all four sides have had a turn. Remove from the oven and leave until to cool enough to handle.

Peel the husks off the corn and trim the ends. Cut each cob in half, into two smaller cobs, to make them easier to handle. With the corn on its side, place your knife in one of the lines in between two rows of kernels, then slowly cut around the cob that way. By doing this you end up with all perfect kernels — not those unsightly little pieces that cutting straight down produces.

FOR THE CHIPOTLE SAUCE

Melt the butter in a saucepan over medium heat. Stir in the flour and cook for 2 minutes, until it just begins to smell nutty but has not coloured. Add the milk and stir constantly until it begins to boil. Reduce the heat and simmer for 5–10 minutes, or until the flour taste has cooked out and the sauce has thickened a little. This sauce isn't very thick, so don't worry — just keep stirring so the bottom doesn't burn. Stir in the cheese and chipotle. Season with sea salt and freshly ground black pepper.

FOR THE MACARONI

Bring a large saucepan of salted water to the boil. Add the pasta, stir, then cook according to the directions on the packet. Once the pasta is just al dente, drain in a colander.

TO SERVE

Heat the ghee in a large non-stick frying pan over medium–high heat. Add the corn and season with salt and pepper. Cook for 2 minutes, then add the macaroni and cook for another 2 minutes. Stir in enough chipotle sauce so the pasta is well coated but not sloppy. Heat through and check the seasoning.

Toss the chives through. Finally, stir the mozzarella through. Serve immediately, in a large bowl.

SERVES 4 AS PART OF A SHARED MEAL

EARTH

GREEN BEAN, TOMATO, OLIVE & FETA SALAD

— ½ red onion, finely sliced
— 35 ml (1¼ fl oz) red wine vinegar
— 500 g (1 lb 2 oz) green beans, the smaller the better
— 4 ripe tomatoes, quartered, seeds removed, then the flesh cut into strips
— 100 g (3½ oz) kalamata olives
— 250 g (9 oz) good-quality feta, cut into cubes
— 100 ml (3½ fl oz) extra virgin olive oil

This is a lovely fresh and crunchy summer salad. We eat this one a lot at home. It goes well with anything — especially fish such as snapper. The best part is soaking up the juices with some crusty sourdough!

Toss the onion in a small bowl with the vinegar and set aside.

Bring a saucepan of salted water to the boil. Remove the stalk end of the beans, then place gently into the boiling water. Cook until just done but still crunchy — usually 2–3 minutes after the water comes back to the boil. Remove from the water and refresh in iced water.

Once cold, remove the beans and drain well on paper towel. Cut each bean diagonally through the centre and place in a large mixing bowl.

Add all the remaining ingredients and toss together. Season with sea salt and freshly ground black pepper.

Serve in a large bowl or on a platter.

SERVES 4 AS PART OF A SHARED MEAL

SOAK UP
THE JUICES
WITH CRUSTY
SOURDOUGH

SALAD OF QUINOA, CHICKPEAS, MUNG BEAN SPROUTS, BEETROOT & SHANKLISH

- 100 g (3½ oz) dried chickpeas, soaked in cold water overnight, then drained
- pinch of bicarbonate of soda (baking soda)
- 200 g (7 oz/1 cup) quinoa, prepared as directed on page 117
- 200 g (7 oz) shanklish (see Note)
- 150 g (5½ oz) mixed sprouts
- 1 golden baby beetroot (beet), sliced into thin rounds
- 1 red baby beetroot (beet), sliced into thin rounds
- 2 radishes, sliced into thin rounds
- 1 tablespoon za'atar (see Note on page 114)
- 100 ml (3½ fl oz) extra virgin olive oil
- 30 ml (1 fl oz) lemon juice
- 12 mint leaves, washed

Place the chickpeas and bicarbonate of soda in a saucepan of salted cold water and bring to the boil. Reduce the heat and simmer for 30–45 minutes, or until the chickpeas are tender, but still holding their shape. Drain in a colander, then tip onto a tray to cool at room temperature.

Toss the cooked quinoa in a large mixing bowl with all the other ingredients, tearing the mint as you add it.

Season to taste with sea salt and freshly ground black pepper.

Serve in a large bowl, or piled on a platter.

SERVES 4 AS PART OF A SHARED MEAL

SHANKLISH IS A DRY, CRUMBLY LEVANTINE CHEESE MADE FROM COW'S OR SHEEP'S MILK. ABOUT THE SIZE OF A TENNIS BALL, IT IS MIXED WITH ALEPPO PEPPER, THEN HUNG AND FINALLY ROLLED WITH ZA'ATAR. LOOK FOR IT IN MIDDLE EASTERN FOOD STORES.

HONEY-ROASTED CARROTS WITH GOAT'S CURD, ZA'ATAR & POMEGRANATE

- 12 baby carrots
- 6 purple baby carrots
- 6 white baby carrots
- 100 g (3½ oz) honey
- 100 ml (3½ fl oz) olive oil
- 200 g (7 oz) goat's curd
- 1 pomegranate, seeded
  (see method on page 110)
- 2 tablespoons za'atar
  (see Note on page 114)
- 50 ml (1¾ fl oz) extra virgin
  olive oil

Baby carrots are naturally so sweet, but they do go really well with honey too. We roast the carrots slowly to enhance that sweetness and to ensure they and the honey don't burn. The tanginess of the goat's curd and pomegranate works perfectly with the carrots. The warm carrots will 'melt' the curd a bit, which makes it even more luxurious. I would suggest serving this with some warm crusty sourdough or pide (Turkish bread) to mop up all the goodness left on the platter. This is happy food!

Preheat the oven to 150°C (300°F).

Trim the carrot greens, leaving 1 cm (½ inch) of the stalks attached. Soak in a large bowl of cold water to remove any dirt left in the stalks. Remove all the carrots from the water, then place in a colander under running water to remove any last bits of dirt. (Make sure you remove the carrots from the water, rather than pouring them straight into a colander, as all the dirt that has sunk to the bottom of the bowl will wash back over them.)

Dry the carrots as thoroughly as possible with paper towel. Place in a large bowl and toss with the honey, olive oil and some sea salt and freshly ground black pepper. Tip the mixture into a large roasting tin, spreading the carrots out in one layer so they cook evenly. Roast for 1 hour, turning every 10 minutes or so.

When the carrots are almost done, get a large platter and smear the goat's curd around the middle of it, so it is covered, but not too thick.

Place the carrots on top of and over the edges of the curd. Sprinkle the pomegranate seeds, za'atar and olive oil over the carrots.

Sprinkle with a little more sea salt and serve.

SERVES 4 AS PART OF A SHARED MEAL

SLOW-ROASTED CRUSHED POTATOES & GARLIC

— 1 kg (2 lb 3 oz) small roasting potatoes, such as nicola or king edward, washed well
— 20 garlic cloves, skinned and brown end bits removed
— 200 ml (7 fl oz) extra virgin olive oil

This is my version of roast potatoes — another dish that is popular at our house. The secret is good-quality potatoes and olive oil. The trick to these potatoes is that when you break them up with your hands, make sure you have bits of all different sizes, so that when they're cooked some are crispy and some are soft. They're excellent for soaking up sauces.

Preheat the oven to 175°C (345°F).

Place the potatoes in a large saucepan of salted cold water. Bring to a boil, then reduce the heat and simmer for 30 minutes, or until soft. Drain in a colander and leave to cool.

Crush the potatoes with your hands into a large bowl, leaving some chunks the size of a walnut shell, and others smaller than that.

Add the garlic cloves and olive oil and toss together. Season with sea salt and freshly ground black pepper and toss again.

Place the potatoes in a roasting tin, spreading them evenly in one layer. Roast for 40–50 minutes, or until golden and crisp, turning every 15 minutes.

Serve hot, in a large bowl.

SERVES 4 AS PART OF A SHARED MEAL

MAKE SURE YOU
HAVE BITS OF ALL
DIFFERENT SIZES,
SO WHEN THEY'RE
COOKED SOME ARE
CRISPY AND SOME
ARE SOFT!

EARTH

CHARGRILLED ASPARAGUS WITH PARMESAN LEMON DRESSING & BRIOCHE-CRUMBED EGG

- 20 asparagus spears
- 50 ml (1¾ fl oz) white wine vinegar
- 4 free-range eggs
- vegetable oil, for deep-frying
- lemon-infused extra virgin olive oil, for tossing
- parmesan cheese, for shaving

PARMESAN LEMON DRESSING

- 2 eggs, at room temperature
- 1 tablespoon dijon mustard
- 100 ml (3½ fl oz) lemon juice
- 50 g (1¾ oz/½ cup) grated parmesan
- 300 ml (10 fl oz) olive oil

CONTINUES OPPOSITE →

Spring is a wonderful time of year for food. Asparagus is one of the delights that defines this season. You have to make sure that you get your fill when it's around, because it's gone again in a flash! This is my version of some of the classic flavours that go well with asparagus. Blanching the asparagus before cooking really helps it stay plump and juicy. We use Parmigiano Reggiano parmesan, as it is hard to go past the best.

FOR THE PARMESAN LEMON DRESSING

Bring a small saucepan of salted water to the boil and gently add the whole eggs. Cook for 3 minutes, then cool the eggs in iced water.

Shell the eggs and add to a food processor with the mustard, lemon juice and parmesan. Blitz together, then add the olive oil in a slow, steady stream to make a rich, creamy, emulsified dressing. Season with sea salt and freshly ground black pepper. Cover and refrigerate until required; the dressing can be made several days ahead.

FOR THE ASPARAGUS

Trim the asparagus stems, so the spears are about 12 cm (4¾ inches) long. Test that you have cut the woody part away by slicing a small disc from the end and tasting it. (I think the 'snapping' method is a load of rubbish, because the asparagus will snap depending on how you are holding it, not necessarily where the woody bit ends.) Lightly peel the asparagus — or if it is young and tender, there is no need.

Bring a saucepan of salted water to the boil. Add the asparagus and cook for 4–5 minutes, or until just tender, but still crisp. Remove and refresh in iced water. Once cool, drain on paper towel and set aside.

TO POACH THE EGGS

Bring a saucepan of salted water to poaching temperature (just below simmering point — there should be no movement in the water, maybe just a few bubbles on the bottom of the pan). Add the vinegar. Crack the eggs into a cup, then gently slide them into the water. Cook for 3–4 minutes, until the whites are firm, but the yolks are still runny. Remove using a slotted spoon and place in a bowl of iced water to stop the eggs cooking any further. Remove from the iced water and drain on paper towel.

Continues opposite →

**CONTINUED FROM
PREVIOUS PAGE** →

BRIOCHE CRUMBS

— ½ loaf day-old brioche,
  from a good baker, diced
— 1 egg
— 100 ml (3½ fl oz) milk
— plain (all-purpose) flour,
  for dusting

FOR THE BRIOCHE CRUMBS

Pulse the brioche in a clean, dry food processor until you have a mix of coarse and fine crumbs. Set aside.

In a bowl, whisk the egg and milk together well.

Dust the poached eggs in the flour, then pass through the egg wash, then coat with the brioche crumbs. Repeat the egg wash and brioche crumbs, pressing the crumbs on to make a good crust. Place in the fridge to set for 1 hour.

TO FINISH THE DISH

Heat about 5 cm (2 inches) of vegetable oil in a medium-sized saucepan to 180°C (355°F). Test by dipping a wooden chopstick into the oil: the chopstick will sizzle when the oil is ready.

Meanwhile, also heat a cast-iron grill plate (or barbecue) to high.

Toss the asparagus with a little lemon olive oil and some sea salt and freshly ground black pepper. Cook on the grill for 4–5 minutes, or until it has good grill marks on it, and is hot but not overcooked or burnt. Toss it with a little of the parmesan lemon dressing to coat.

Gently lower the crumbed eggs into the oil and cook for 2 minutes, or until golden brown. You want the crumbs to be cooked, but the yolk to be runny. Remove with a slotted spoon and immediately drain on paper towel. Season with salt and pepper.

TO SERVE

Arrange the asparagus on plates or a large platter and drizzle with more of the parmesan lemon dressing.

Plop the crumbed eggs on top, then use a vegetable peeler to shave more parmesan over the whole dish. Serve straight away.

SERVES 4 AS PART OF A SHARED MEAL

EARTH

PARMESAN LEMON
DRESSING

BRIOCHE-
CRUMBED EGG

SEA SALT &
BLACK PEPPER,
FOR SEASONING

TOMATO, BUFFALO MOZZARELLA & BASIL SALAD

- 6 mixed heirloom tomatoes
- 250 g (9 oz) buffalo mozzarella
- 1 handful basil cress, snipped
- 1 handful purple basil cress, snipped
- 50 ml (1¾ fl oz) good-quality red wine vinegar
- 100 ml (3½ fl oz) extra virgin olive oil

Insalata caprese is one of my favourite salads. This is my version. To make this salad you must use the best tomatoes — heirloom preferably — you can find during their season in summer! I use locally made buffalo mozzarella, but there is no shortage of options, with literally tonnes of Italian 'mozzarella di bufala' being air-freighted around the globe every week. If you can't find basil cress, use basil leaves, torn into large pieces. Serve with crusty sourdough for mopping up those delicious juices.

Slice the tomatoes about 5 mm (¼ inch) thick, or in half if very small. Tear the mozzarella into smaller chunks.

On a large serving platter, arrange the tomatoes, mozzarella and basil cresses so they are all overlapping, seasoning generously with sea salt and freshly ground black pepper along the way.

Drizzle the vinegar, then the olive oil, over everything and add another sprinkling of salt and pepper.

SERVES 4 AS PART OF A SHARED MEAL

USE HEIRLOOM
TOMATOES IF YOU
CAN FIND THEM

EARTH

ROASTED BRUSSELS SPROUTS & PORTOBELLO MUSHROOMS

- 4 large portobello mushrooms
- 100 ml (3½ fl oz) olive oil
- 100 g (3½ oz) butter, diced
- 6 thyme sprigs, picked and chopped
- 2 garlic cloves, crushed
- 50 ml (1¾ fl oz) sherry vinegar
- 500 g (1 lb 2 oz) brussels sprouts
- 150 g (5½ oz) ghee (clarified butter), melted

I love brussels sprouts when they are roasted. Their caramelisation is just delicious, and pairs wonderfully with the earthiness of the mushrooms. This dish goes especially well with the Red wine braised short ribs with parsnip purée on page 96.

Preheat the oven to 180°C (355°F) and line a baking tray with baking paper.

Peel each mushroom and slice the stalk so it is flush with the gills. Place the mushrooms on the baking tray, gill side up. Drizzle with the olive oil, then distribute the butter, thyme and garlic evenly between them. Roast for 15–20 minutes, until the mushrooms are fully cooked, but not dried out. Drizzle with the vinegar and set aside to cool.

Cut the bases off the brussels sprouts, then cut the sprouts in half, from the bottom. Remove any tough outer leaves. Place a small cut in the thick part of the core.

Heat a large non-stick ovenproof frying pan over medium heat and add the ghee. One by one, add the brussels sprouts to the pan, cut side down. Cook for 7–8 minutes, until nicely browned, checking frequently to see that they are turning golden but are not getting burnt. Turn them over once and season with sea salt and freshly ground black pepper.

Transfer the pan to the oven and bake the brussels sprouts for 10 minutes or so, tossing occasionally.

Cut each mushroom into 6–8 large wedges, then add them to the brussels sprouts. Roast for another 5 minutes, then check to make sure the sprouts are cooked in the middle.

Check the seasoning and serve immediately, in a bowl.

SERVES 4 AS PART OF A SHARED MEAL

LIGHTLY PICKLED BABY BEETROOT
WITH HUMMUS, DILL OIL & TOASTED RYE

- 6 red baby beetroot (beets)
- 6 golden baby beetroot (beets)
- 6 candy-stripe baby beetroot (beets)
- 150 ml (5 fl oz) white wine vinegar
- 150 g (5½ oz) sugar
- 1 tablespoon black peppercorns
- 3 bay leaves
- 150 ml (5 fl oz) chardonnay vinegar
- 150 ml (5 fl oz) extra virgin olive oil
- 100 ml (3½ fl oz) red wine vinegar
- Hummus (page 180), to serve
- Dill oil (page 179), for drizzling

RYE CRUMBS

- ½ loaf dark rye bread (100% rye)
- 50 ml (1¾ fl oz) olive oil
- 1 teaspoon caraway seeds

Beetroot is one of my favourite vegetables. For this dish it's great if you can get some golden and candy-striped beets. The toasted dark rye bread gives a great crunch.

Trim the stalks off the beetroot; wash and reserve the stalks. Wash the beetroot well and soak in cold water for 10 minutes to dislodge any sand or dirt.

Place each beetroot variety in a separate saucepan and cover with water. Add 50 ml (1¾ fl oz) of the white wine vinegar, 50 g (1¾ oz) of the sugar, 1 teaspoon of the peppercorns, a bay leaf and a pinch of sea salt to each pan and bring to a gentle boil. Cook over medium heat for about 20 minutes, until just tender, then drain.

While the beetroot are still warm, slip off the skins, wearing latex gloves. Trim the ends to ensure they are neat. Toss with the chardonnay vinegar, olive oil and some sea salt and freshly ground black pepper and set aside.

Cut the beetroot stalks and leaves into 3 mm (⅛ inch) slices, then toss with the red wine vinegar and some salt and pepper. Cover and leave in the fridge to pickle for at least 1 day, or up to 1 week.

FOR THE RYE CRUMBS

Preheat the oven to 160°C (320°F) and line a tray with baking paper.

Remove the crust from the bread. Cut the bread into large cubes. Place in a food processor with the olive oil, caraway seeds and some salt and pepper. Pulse until there is a mix of large and small chunks.

Place the crumbs on the baking tray and bake for 40–50 minutes, or until the crumbs are crisp. Leave to cool, then transfer to an airtight container; the crumbs will keep for several days.

TO SERVE

Spread the hummus in the bottom of a bowl or platter. Top with the beetroot, making sure to distribute the different colours. Scatter the pickled beetroot stalks and leaves around. Drizzle with the dill oil, then scatter liberally with the rye crumbs.

Garnish with the reserved dill tips and serve.

SERVES 4 AS PART OF A SHARED MEAL

EARTH

SALAD OF SHAVED FENNEL, POMEGRANATE, GOAT'S CHEESE & BLOOD ORANGE

— 2 blood oranges
— 25 ml (¾ fl oz) good-quality white wine vinegar
— 150 ml (5 fl oz) extra virgin olive oil
— 2 large fennel bulbs
— 1 pomegranate, seeded (see method on page 110)
— 200 g (7 oz) marinated goat's cheese
— 6 mint sprigs, picked

Fennel is another of my favourite vegetables, and I much prefer it raw to cooked. When shaved, it makes a great salad ingredient, and goes really well with orange — in this case blood orange.

To segment the oranges, cut off the tops and bottoms using a small sharp knife. Working with one orange at a time, sit the orange on its flat bottom, then use the knife to cut away the skin and white pith, cutting from top to bottom, all the way around the orange.

Working over a bowl to catch any juices, use the knife to cut between the fruit and the connective membrane of one orange segment. Cut the membrane off the other side, to release the orange segment, keeping the membrane as clean as possible. Squeeze the membranes over the bowl, to catch any juices. Cut the remaining orange segments in the same way, reserving any juices that fall into the bowl.

Mix the reserved orange juice with the vinegar and olive oil.

Trim the base of the fennel and remove any old outer pieces. Trim the stalks off the top and give them a wash to make sure there's no dirt.

Shave the fennel very thinly, until you reach the core, using a mandoline. (Be very careful not to slice your fingers, as this is the piece of equipment I have seen cause the most amount of kitchen injuries!) Do this just before serving, or the fennel will discolour and dry out. Some people like to shave it, then put it in water, but all this does is wash the flavour away.

Place the fennel in a large bowl. Add all the other ingredients, tearing up the mint as you go. Toss all the ingredients together and season with sea salt and freshly ground black pepper.

Serve in a large bowl.

SERVES 4 AS PART OF A SHARED MEAL

A BRIGHT,
VIBRANT SALAD!

SWEET

SILKEN CHOCOLATE MOUSSE WITH MARCONA ALMONDS & RASPBERRY SAUCE

— 400 g (14 oz) dark chocolate
— 8 eggs, separated
— 200 g (7 oz) butter, diced and softened
— 1½ tablespoons caster (superfine) sugar
— 20 g (¾ oz) freeze-dried raspberry powder (see Note)
— 120 g (4½ oz) chopped salted marcona almonds (see Note)

RASPBERRY SAUCE

— 250 g (9 oz) frozen raspberries, thawed
— 125 g (4½ oz) sugar
— juice of ½ lemon

This was on the first menu at Huxtable. The mousse recipe is inspired by one from the Australian cooking legend Stephanie Alexander. I love the rich, dense fudgy texture mixed with the slight acidity of the raspberry sauce and the nutty crunch of the almonds.

FOR THE MOUSSE

Spray a 28 cm (11 inch), 1.5 litre (51 fl oz/6 cup) terrine mould with cooking oil spray and line with baking paper.

Place the chocolate in a heatproof bowl. Set the bowl over a saucepan of simmering water, ensuring the base of the bowl does not touch the water. Gently melt the chocolate, stirring until smooth. Remove from the heat, then beat in the egg yolks, one at a time. Add the butter and beat until glossy and smooth.

Whip the egg whites in a large clean bowl until soft peaks form. Sprinkle the caster sugar over and continue to whip until the egg whites are satiny.

• MARCONA ALMONDS ARE FROM A SPECIFIC REGION IN SPAIN. THEY ARE FLATTER AND ROUNDER THAN NORMAL ALMONDS, AND SLIGHTLY SWEETER. IF YOU CAN'T FIND THEM, USE REGULAR SALTED, ROASTED ALMONDS.

Gently but thoroughly fold the chocolate mixture through the egg whites. The mixture may look like it has split, but just hold your nerve and keep mixing — it will come back together. Pour into the lined mould, cover with plastic wrap and refrigerate overnight.

FOR THE RASPBERRY SAUCE

Place the raspberries, sugar and lemon juice in a saucepan. Bring to a simmer and stir until well mixed and the sugar has dissolved. Strain through a fine strainer, into a container. Cover and place in the fridge to chill.

TO SERVE

Remove the terrine mould from the fridge, then tip it upside down on a chopping board to remove the mousse. You may need to slightly warm the outside of the mould with a kitchen blowtorch or hot damp cloth — just make sure you don't melt the mousse!

Pour a small pool of raspberry sauce onto each plate. Using a hot knife, cut into slices around 2 cm (¾ inch) thick. Place one slice on each plate, along one edge of the raspberry sauce. Sprinkle the raspberry powder over the mousse. Arrange a line of chopped almonds across each plate and serve.

• FREEZE-DRIED RASPBERRY POWDER CAN BE FOUND AT SPECIALTY PASTRY STORES. IT SHOULD BE STORED IN THE FRIDGE. HANDLE WITH DRY FINGERS, OR YOU'LL END UP WITH RED, STICKY HANDS!

SERVES 10–14

PLACE THE CHOCOLATE
MOUSSE ON A POOL OF
RASPBERRY SAUCE

WARM JAM-FILLED
DOUGHNUTS ON
A SILKY SMEAR OF
ORANGE BLOSSOM
CUSTARD

RHUBARB JAM DOUGHNUTS WITH ORANGE BLOSSOM CUSTARD & YOGHURT SORBET

— 1 litre (34 fl oz/4 cups) vegetable oil, for deep-frying
— caster (superfine) sugar, for dusting
— Yoghurt sorbet (page 203), to serve
— Rhubarb crisps (page 194), to serve
— snipped lemon balm cress, to garnish

DOUGHNUTS

— 230 ml (8 fl oz) milk
— 28 g (1 oz) fresh yeast, or 56 g (2 oz) dried yeast
— 650 g (1 lb 7 oz) plain (all-purpose) flour
— 2 scant teaspoons sea salt
— 50 g (1¾ oz) caster (superfine) sugar
— 1 large egg (75 g/2¾ oz)
— 2 egg yolks
— 3 teaspoons maple syrup
— 75 g (2¾ oz) butter, diced and softened
— 1 quantity Rhubarb jam (page 194; enjoy the leftovers on toast!)

CONTINUES OVERLEAF →

When Krista Corbett, one of our very talented chefs, came up with this dish, it pretty much blew my socks off. The flavours and textures are just awesome. Unfortunately there would always be extra doughnuts appearing in the kitchen, which we would have to devour!

FOR THE DOUGHNUTS

Heat the milk to 38°C (100°F) in a saucepan. Whisk in the yeast, then place in the bowl of an electric mixer with a dough hook attached. Add the flour, salt and sugar. Begin mixing on low speed, then gradually add the egg, egg yolks, maple syrup and butter.

Cover the dough and leave to prove in a warm, draught-free area for 30 minutes to 1 hour, or until doubled in size.

Knock back the dough by lightly punching it, then shape into eighteen 20 g (¾ oz) balls (you may want to do a few extra for 'tasters'; you can store any left-over dough in the freezer for another day).

Place on a floured tray, lightly cover with a clean cloth and leave to rise for about 1 hour, or until doubled in size again.

Put some of the rhubarb jam in a disposable piping (icing) bag, or a disposable large syringe from a chemist. Set aside.

Continues overleaf →

CONTINUED FROM
PREVIOUS PAGE ↖

ORANGE BLOSSOM CUSTARD

- 225 ml (7½ fl oz) pouring (single/light) cream
- 45 g (1½ oz) caster (superfine) sugar
- zest of 1 orange
- 3 egg yolks
- 2 teaspoons Cointreau or other orange-flavoured liqueur
- dash of orange blossom water

FOR THE ORANGE BLOSSOM CUSTARD

Combine the cream, sugar and orange zest in a small saucepan and slowly infuse over low heat for 30 minutes.

Combine the egg yolks and liqueur in a bowl. Slowly strain the cream into the egg yolks, constantly whisking to combine. Pour the mixture into a clean heatproof bowl, then heat over a saucepan of just-simmering water until curdled and split — this will take 30–40 minutes.

Transfer to a blender and blitz well, scraping down the side, until the mixture is smooth and shiny. Pour into a container and refrigerate for about 1 hour, or until the custard has set.

Once set, transfer the custard to a large bowl and whisk in a little orange blossom water to taste (be careful, the flavour is very strong!). Pour into a container and refrigerate until required.

TO SERVE

Heat the vegetable oil in a large saucepan to 180°C (355°F). Test by dipping a wooden chopstick into the oil: the chopstick will sizzle when the oil is ready.

Gently drop the doughnuts into the hot oil, being careful to not overcrowd the pan; a good rule of thumb is that only two-thirds of the oil surface should be covered with doughnuts. Once golden on one side, flip them over to brown the other side. They may try and misbehave, but you just have to stand over them with a stern look and keep rolling them back.

Once golden all over, drain on paper towel, then toss them in a bowl of caster sugar. Use the piping bag or syringe to inject jam into the middle of each doughnut. Keep the doughnuts warm until all are done.

Meanwhile, prepare six plates or bowls and plop a decent spoonful of custard on one side of each. Using the back of the spoon, smear the custard into interesting shapes.

Arrange three warm doughnuts on one side of the custard, then add a scoop of sorbet next to them. Top the sorbet with a rhubarb crisp, sprinkle with lemon balm cress and serve.

SERVES 6

CHERRY, PISTACHIO & CHOCOLATE TRIFLE

- 500 g (1 lb 2 oz) cherries, halved and pitted
- 5 gelatine leaves, soaked in cold water
- 1 Chocolate genoise sponge (page 190), broken into large pieces
- 100 ml (3½ fl oz) Pedro Ximénez sherry (see Note)
- 75 g (2¾ oz/½ cup) blanched, peeled and roasted pistachios, chopped
- 60 g (2 oz/½ cup) grated dark chocolate

POACHING LIQUID

- 250 ml (8½ fl oz/1 cup) water
- 200 ml (7 fl oz) Pedro Ximénez sherry (see Note)
- 50 ml (1¾ fl oz) Luxardo Maraschino cherry liqueur (see Note)
- 2 star anise
- ½ cinnamon stick
- 100 g (3½ oz) sugar

PISTACHIO CUSTARD

- 125 ml (4 fl oz/½ cup) milk
- 125 ml (4 fl oz/½ cup) pouring (single/light) cream
- ½ vanilla bean, split lengthways and seeds scraped
- 7 egg yolks
- 100 g (3½ oz) sugar
- 2 tablespoons pistachio nut paste (available from good Italian grocers and pastry stores)

I absolutely love cherries! When they're in season I always eat as many as possible. They go really well with pistachios and chocolate. This is a great dessert because you can make it earlier in the day and let all the flavours come together.

FOR THE CHERRIES

Combine the poaching liquid ingredients in a saucepan and bring to a simmer. Turn off the heat and let steep for 30 minutes.

Return the poaching liquid to poaching temperature (just below simmering point — there should be no movement in the liquid, maybe just a few bubbles on the bottom of the pan). Add the cherries, then cover with a round of baking paper and a side plate to keep the cherries submerged. Gently poach for 10–15 minutes, or until tender. Leave to cool.

PEDRO XIMÉNEZ IS AN INTENSELY SWEET, DARK DESSERT SHERRY FROM SPAIN.

Warm 500 ml (17 fl oz/2 cups) of the poaching liquid and dissolve the gelatine in it. Strain into a container and refrigerate for at least 2 hours to set. Once set, dice the jelly into 2 cm (¾ inch) cubes.

LUXARDO MARASCHINO IS AN ITALIAN SOUR-CHERRY LIQUEUR, MATURED FOR 2 YEARS IN FINNISH ASH VATS.

FOR THE PISTACHIO CUSTARD

In a saucepan, scald the milk and cream over medium heat with the vanilla pod and vanilla seeds.

Meanwhile, whisk the egg yolks with the sugar until the sugar has dissolved.

As soon as the milk mixture has scalded, immediately pour it over the egg yolk mixture. Pour the mixture back into the saucepan and stir constantly over low heat for 8–10 minutes, until the mixture is thick.

Strain the custard into a bowl, through a fine sieve. Mix in the pistachio paste. Set the bowl over an iced water bath, stirring from time to time, until cooled. Cover and refrigerate until needed; the custard can be made a day ahead.

TO ASSEMBLE

Place a layer of cake pieces in the bottom of a glass bowl or bowls, then sprinkle with a little sherry. Top with a layer of custard, then some cherry jelly cubes. Repeat the layers until all the ingredients have been used. Serve topped with the pistachios and grated chocolate.

SERVES 6

SWEET

143

MANDARIN CRÈME BRÛLÉE WITH CARDAMOM LANGUES DE CHAT

LANGUES DE CHAT

— 100 g (3½ oz) butter, diced
— 80 g (2¾ oz) icing (confectioners') sugar
— zest of 1 orange
— 3 egg whites
— 100 g (3½ oz) plain (all-purpose) flour, sifted
— seeds from 8 cardamom pods, toasted and ground

CRÈME BRÛLÉE

— 900 ml (30½ fl oz) pouring (single/light) cream
— 175 g (6 oz) caster (superfine) sugar, plus extra, for sprinkling
— zest of 8 mandarins
— 15 egg yolks
— 30 ml (1 fl oz) Mandarine Napoléon, or other mandarin-flavoured liqueur
— 24 mandarin segments

Crème brûlée is so rich and decadent. I love the flavour of mandarin, a perfect match for cardamom. This method is a 'no-bake' one. You essentially cook out the custard until it splits, then blend to bring it back together. Don't be scared — it's more foolproof than baking!

FOR THE LANGUES DE CHAT

Preheat the oven to 180°C (355°F) and line a baking tray with baking paper.

Cream the butter, icing sugar and orange zest in a food processor. Add the egg whites one at a time, until thoroughly combined, then scrape the mixture into a bowl. Sift the flour and cardamom over and stir until just combined.

Put the dough in a disposable piping (icing) bag. Pipe 16 thin lines onto the baking paper, into 8 cm (3¼ inch) lengths. Bake for 5–10 minutes, until browned evenly on the outside and bottom. Cool on the baking tray and store in an airtight container for up to 1 week.

FOR THE CRÈME BRÛLÉE

Combine the cream, sugar and mandarin zest in a saucepan and slowly infuse over low heat for 30 minutes.

In a large bowl, lightly whisk the egg yolks and liqueur. Slowly strain the warm cream into the egg yolks, constantly whisking to combine. Pour the mixture into a clean bowl and heat over a large saucepan of just-simmering water, stirring occasionally, until curdled and split — this will take 30–45 minutes.

Pour the hot mixture into a blender in small amounts and blitz well, scraping down the side, until the mixture is smooth and shiny.

Have ready eight 200 ml (7 fl oz) brûlée moulds and arrange three mandarin segments in each. Pour in the custard mixture. Firmly tap the moulds on the bench to release the air bubbles, then smooth the surface. Refrigerate, uncovered, for at least 8 hours or overnight, to set and get a dry crust on top.

TO SERVE

Evenly sprinkle some caster sugar over the top of each set custard, until just covered. Scrape around the sides of the moulds with your thumb to clean away any excess sugar. Use a kitchen blow torch to gently go back and forth across the sugar, until it is all melted and slightly darker than golden brown, but not burnt.

Serve immediately, with two biscuits per person to dip into the custard.

SERVES 8

ENCOURAGE YOUR
GUESTS TO DIP THE
LANGUES DE CHAT,
OR 'CAT'S TONGUES',
INTO THE CREAM

SWEET

145

DOT WITH STRAWBERRY
PEARLS AND GARNISH
WITH BASIL CRESS

CRÈME FRAÎCHE CHEESECAKE WITH STRAWBERRIES, CITRUS CRUMBS & STRAWBERRY SORBET

- Lemon gel (page 192), to serve
- Strawberry sorbet (page 203), to serve
- Strawberry crisps (page 195), to serve
- snipped basil cress, to garnish

CHEESECAKE MIX

- 200 g (7 oz) cream cheese
- zest and juice of 1 lemon
- ½ vanilla bean, split lengthways and seeds scraped
- 125 g (4½ oz) caster (superfine) sugar
- 250 g (9 oz) crème fraîche

BASIL-MACERATED STRAWBERRIES

- 250 g (9 oz) strawberries, washed, hulled and quartered
- 1 tablespoon sparkling wine
- 2 tablespoons caster (superfine) sugar
- 6 large basil leaves, torn
- 2 basil stems, bruised

CITRUS CRUMBS

- 150 g (5½ oz/1 cup) plain (all-purpose) flour
- 45 g (1½ oz) icing (confectioners') sugar, sifted
- 125 g (4½ oz) butter, diced
- zest of 2 limes
- zest of 1 lemon
- pinch of sea salt

CONTINUES OVERLEAF →

This is a very light and fresh summery dessert. I love the creaminess of the cheesecake. All the flavours and textures of cheesecake are there — just not how you would expect.

FOR THE CHEESECAKE MIX

Dice the cream cheese and bring to room temperature. Add to a food processor with the lemon zest, lemon juice, vanilla seeds and sugar. Blitz well, scraping down the side of the processor, until smooth. Pass the mixture through a fine strainer, into a large bowl.

In a separate bowl, whip the crème fraîche using a hand whisk until stiff peaks form. Fold a small amount into the cream cheese mixture until well combined, then fold in the rest of the whipped crème fraîche. Spoon into a container, then cover and set in the refrigerator overnight.

FOR THE BASIL-MACERATED STRAWBERRIES

Place all the ingredients in a bowl and gently combine. Cover and leave to sit overnight in the fridge.

FOR THE CITRUS CRUMBS

Combine all the ingredients in a food processor and blitz until combined. Turn out onto a bench and lightly knead into a log. Roll in plastic wrap and rest in the fridge for 30 minutes, or until firm.

Roll the dough out to about 3 mm (⅛ inch) thick between two sheets of baking paper. Rest in the fridge for at least another 30 minutes. Meanwhile, preheat the oven to 160°C (320°F).

Place the dough on a baking tray and bake for 10–15 minutes, until lightly golden and crisp. Leave to cool, then blitz quickly in a food processor until crumbs form. Store at room temperature in a clean, dry container; the crumbs can be made a day ahead.

Continues overleaf →

SWEET

**CONTINUED FROM
PREVIOUS PAGE ⬉**

STRAWBERRY PEARLS

- 500 ml (17 fl oz/2 cups) cottonseed oil
- 150 g (5½ oz) strawberries, washed and hulled
- 20 g (¾ oz) caster (superfine) sugar
- juice of ¼ lemon
- 2 gelatine leaves, soaked in iced water

FOR THE STRAWBERRY PEARLS

Pour the cottonseed oil into a container, then chill in the freezer for 2 hours, so the oil is as cold as possible.

Blend the strawberries with the sugar and lemon juice until smooth, then pass through a fine strainer. Warm a small amount of the strawberry purée in a saucepan. Stir in the soaked gelatine until dissolved, then add the gelatine mixture to the remaining strawberry purée. Pass through a fine sieve.

Use a disposable syringe from the chemist to drop small amounts of the strawberry liquid into the cold oil. Leave the strawberry pearls to set in the fridge for at least 30 minutes. Once set, strain through a fine sieve, then wash in iced water until all the oil is washed off the pearls.

Place the pearls in a container lined with baking paper. Store in the fridge until required; the pearls can be made a day or two ahead.

TO SERVE

Sprinkle some citrus crumbs along the middle of six plates (you won't need all the crumbs, so reserve these for another use).

Using a hot spoon, scoop out egg-shaped 'quenelles' from the cheesecake mix, placing two quenelles evenly along the crumbs on each plate.

Evenly distribute the macerated strawberries out along the crumbs. Arrange some of the strawberry pearls along the crumbs.

Place a few dots of lemon gel in and around the crumbs. Finally, place a scoop of the sorbet at one end of the crumbs, then scatter the strawberry crisps and some basil cress along the whole dessert. Sit down and enjoy!

SERVES 6

BANANA FRITTERS WITH COCONUT SORBET, RUM CARAMEL & SESAME WAFERS

— 6 ripe but firm bananas
— Coconut sorbet (page 199),
  to serve
— Sesame wafers (page 188),
  to serve

BATTER

— 75 g (2¾ oz/½ cup)
  self-raising flour
— 30 g (1 oz/¼ cup) cornflour
  (cornstarch)
— 1 tablespoon rice flour
— ½ teaspoon baking powder
— pinch of sugar
— 180 ml (6 fl oz) water
— 1½ tablespoons vegetable oil

RUM CARAMEL

— 125 g (4½ oz) chopped palm
  sugar (jaggery)
— 25 ml (¾ fl oz) golden rum
— 25 ml (¾ fl oz) water
— 1 tablespoon coconut milk
— 20 ml (¾ fl oz) liquid glucose

Banana fritters are a classic at Chinese restaurants. I decided to give them a Thai spin and I am quite partial to rum. These were one of Huxtable's 'simple' desserts in our early days. They sure made the crowd happy!

FOR THE BATTER

Whisk all the ingredients together in a bowl until just combined, being careful not to overmix. Cover and rest in the fridge for 30 minutes.

FOR THE RUM CARAMEL

Combine all the ingredients in a small saucepan. Gently cook until the mixture is smooth and the sugar has dissolved. Continue to cook for 15–20 minutes, until the sauce is thick and syrupy. Cool and keep at room temperature.

TO SERVE

Heat about 5 cm (2 inches) of vegetable oil in a large saucepan to 180°C (355°F). Test by dipping a wooden chopstick into the oil: the chopstick will sizzle when the oil is ready.

Cut the bananas in half across the middle (not lengthways). Using a fork, dip them in the batter. Working in two batches so as not to overcrowd the pan, cook the bananas in the hot oil for 3–4 minutes, or until the batter is crisp and golden.

Spoon a decent amount of the caramel into the bottom of four bowls. Top with three pieces of banana per person. Top each with a scoop of sorbet, then a sesame wafer, and tuck in.

SERVES 4

WHITE CHOCOLATE PANNA COTTA WITH SALTED CARAMEL GANACHE & RASPBERRIES

- 450 g (1 lb) raspberries
- Vanilla tuiles (page 188), to serve
- lemon balm cress, to garnish

PANNA COTTA

- 100 ml (3½ fl oz) milk
- 60 g (2 oz) agave nectar
- 3 gelatine leaves, soaked in iced water
- 120 g (4½ oz) white chocolate, chopped
- 300 ml (10 oz) thickened (whipping) cream
- 100 g (3½ oz) Greek-style yoghurt

GANACHE

- 150 g (5½ oz) sugar
- 35 ml (1¼ fl oz) liquid glucose
- 200 ml (7 fl oz) pouring (single/light) cream
- pinch of sea salt
- 65 g (2¼ oz) cold butter, diced
- 100 g (3½ oz) dark chocolate, chopped

This dessert comes from one of our incredibly talented chefs, Matt Combes. It was very popular when it was on the menu at Huxtable, and despite its simplicity, it is quite complex in flavour.

FOR THE RASPBERRIES

Set two-thirds of the raspberries aside. Break the remaining raspberries into small pieces and place in the freezer on a tray lined with baking paper. Leave to freeze for about 2 hours. Once frozen, pack the raspberries down into a container and reserve in the freezer.

FOR THE PANNA COTTA

In a saucepan, bring the milk and agave nectar to a simmer; add the gelatine and stir to dissolve. Place the chocolate in a large heatproof bowl, add the milk mixture and whisk until well combined. Add the cream and yoghurt and whisk until smooth. Pour the mixture into six 125 ml (4 fl oz/½ cup) dariole moulds, then leave to set in the fridge for a few hours.

FOR THE GANACHE

Put the sugar, glucose and 3 teaspoons water in a saucepan and stir to make a wet 'sand' mixture. Place over medium heat and cook for 10–15 minutes, until golden caramel in colour.

While the sugar mixture is caramelising, gently heat the cream and salt in another saucepan, to just below simmering point.

Once the sugar has caramelised, remove from the heat and carefully whisk in the warm cream mixture — be careful of steam and splatters! Allow to cool slightly, then slowly add the cold butter, a little at a time.

Once all the butter has melted into the salted caramel, slowly add the chocolate and stir until well combined. Set aside.

TO SERVE

Generously smear the ganache on the inside of six bowls, from one side to the other. Gently remove the panna cotta from the moulds and place in the middle. Scatter the reserved fresh raspberries and segments of frozen raspberry over and around. Stick a tuile to the side of each panna cotta, garnish with lemon balm cress and serve.

SERVES 6

A PIMPED VERSION OF AN
OLD-FASHIONED
ICE-CREAM SANDWICH!

ICE-CREAM & FUDGE SANDWICH

— 8 pieces Shortbread
  (page 189), to serve

**VANILLA ANGLAISE
(ICE-CREAM BASE)**

— 500 ml (17 fl oz/2 cups)
  unhomogenised milk
— 500 ml (17 fl oz/2 cups)
  pouring (single/light) cream
— 200 g (7 oz) sugar
— 1 vanilla bean, split lengthways
  and seeds scraped
— 15 egg yolks
— 1 heaped tablespoon liquid
  glucose

CONTINUES OVERLEAF →

I have fond memories of being over at my neighbours', who always had ice-cream slices and pink wafers that fit to make a sandwich. This is my pimped version, which has the centre cut out to allow for chocolate fudge to be piped in. We have had this on the menu since day one and change the flavour with every batch of ice-cream made. The possibilities are endless — just start with the vanilla base and add whatever you like. We usually use dark chocolate fudge, but change it to white chocolate sometimes to complement the ice-cream flavour.

FOR THE VANILLA ANGLAISE

Scald the milk, cream, sugar, vanilla pod and vanilla seeds in a saucepan over medium heat.

Meanwhile, combine the egg yolks and glucose in a large bowl.

Slowly pour the scalded milk into the egg yolk mixture, whisking constantly. Strain the mixture back into the saucepan. Cook over low heat, stirring constantly, until the anglaise becomes thick enough to coat the back of the spoon. Strain immediately into a bowl set over an iced water bath, then stir frequently until cool. Cover and refrigerate overnight.

The next day, churn the mixture in an ice-cream machine according to the manufacturer's instructions. Once churned, spread out on a tray so the mixture is about 1.5 cm (½ inch) thick. Freeze overnight.

The next day, cut out a disc of ice-cream, using a 10 cm (4 inch) ring cutter. Now cut the middle from that ring, using a 3 cm (1¼ inch) cutter. Place the larger outside ring on a tray lined with baking paper and place back in the freezer. Repeat until you have four discs with the centre cut out. (You can save the centre discs for topping other desserts.)

Continues overleaf →

SWEET

CONTINUED FROM
PREVIOUS PAGE →

DARK CHOCOLATE FUDGE

— 105 ml (3½ fl oz) milk
— 90 ml (3 fl oz) pouring (single/light) cream
— 90 ml (3 fl oz) liquid glucose
— 1 tablespoon water
— 200 g (7 oz) dark chocolate, chopped

WHITE CHOCOLATE FUDGE

— 50 ml (1¾ fl oz) pouring (single/light) cream
— 35 ml (1¼ fl oz) milk
— 75 ml (2½ fl oz) liquid glucose
— 2 teaspoons water
— 175 g (6 oz) white chocolate, chopped

FOR THE DARK CHOCOLATE OR WHITE CHOCOLATE FUDGE

Make either the dark or white chocolate fudge, using the following method.

Combine all the ingredients, except the chocolate, in a saucepan and heat until simmering.

Place the chocolate in a food processor. Slowly add the hot liquid, while blitzing to combine. Once combined, scrape down the side and blitz for 1 minute more.

Pour the fudge mixture into a disposable piping (icing) bag. Leave to cool at room temperature, then refrigerate until ready to use. The fudge can be made several days ahead, left in the fridge.

TO SERVE

Look through your shortbread discs and reserve the four best-looking ones to use as tops. Place the other four on separate plates, with the tray side facing upwards. Place an ice-cream disc on each one, then pipe the fudge into the hole in the middle of the ice-cream. Place the other shortbreads on top.

If the ice-cream is really firm (depending how cold your freezer is), you may want to wait for 5 minutes or so before serving.

Most people use a fork and spoon to eat this dessert, but I think the best way to enjoy it is to pick it up!

SERVES 4

•
BEFORE CUTTING THE END OFF THE PIPING (ICING) BAG, SQUISH THE BAG IN YOUR HANDS A LITTLE TO BURST THE AIR BUBBLES AND SMOOTH THE FUDGE.

COCONUT PANNA COTTA
WITH LYCHEE SALAD & MANGO SORBET

— Mango sorbet (page 200),
to serve

PANNA COTTA

— 650 ml (22 fl oz) coconut milk
— 100 g (3½ oz) caster
(superfine) sugar
— 1 vanilla bean, split lengthways
and seeds scraped
— 5 gelatine leaves, softened
in cold water
— 100 ml (3½ fl oz) Malibu or
other coconut-flavoured rum
— 100 ml (3½ fl oz) pouring
(single/light) cream

LYCHEE SALAD

— 2 slices ripe pineapple, core
removed, flesh diced
— 4 lychees, peeled, stoned
and quartered
— ¼ teaspoon black
sesame seeds
— 2 mint leaves, torn
— ½ kaffir lime (makrut) leaf,
julienned as finely as possible

DRESSING

— 50 ml (1¾ fl oz) sugar syrup
(page 195)
— 50 ml (1¾ fl oz) lime juice

FOR THE PANNA COTTA

In a small saucepan, bring the coconut milk, sugar, vanilla pod and vanilla
seeds to the boil. Transfer to a non-porous container, cover and leave in the
fridge overnight to infuse.

The next day, return the mixture to the boil in a clean saucepan, then leave
to cool slightly, before stirring in the softened gelatine, Malibu and cream.

Strain into eight 100 ml (3½ fl oz) dariole moulds, or into wide bowls or
glasses. Cover and refrigerate for several hours, until set; the panna cotta can
be made a day ahead.

TO SERVE

If using moulds, use a palette knife to gently let a bit of air inside the inner
edge of each mould, to release the suction of the panna cotta, then gently
invert onto eight plates or bowls.

Combine the lychee salad ingredients with the combined dressing ingredients.
If serving on plates, arrange some salad on top and around the panna cotta;
if serving in a bowl, scatter the salad over the top.

Place a nice scoop of mango sorbet to the side of the panna cotta if using
plates, or directly on top if serving in bowls.

SERVES 8

SWEET

UPSIDE-DOWN QUINCE CAKES WITH CINNAMON CRUMBLE & ALMOND ICE-CREAM

— Almond ice-cream (page 198), to serve

CINNAMON CRUMBLE

— 125 g (4½ oz/1 cup) crumbled Shortbreads (page 189)
— ½ teaspoon ground cinnamon
— 1 tablespoon caster (superfine) sugar
— 25 g (1 oz/¼ cup) flaked almonds

QUINCE CAKES

— 355 g (12½ oz) caster (superfine) sugar
— 3 poached and sliced quinces, approximately (page 193)
— 175 g (6 oz) butter, diced and softened
— 4 eggs
— 160 g (5½ oz) plain (all-purpose) flour, sifted
— 1 teaspoon baking powder
— 2½ tablespoons almond meal

This is a perfect ending to a winter dinner party. I can attest that these cakes are quite delicious the next day at room temperature too.

FOR THE CINNAMON CRUMBLE

Preheat the oven to 160°C (320°F) and line a baking tray with baking paper.

Combine all the ingredients in a bowl, then evenly spread them out on the baking tray. Bake for 5 minutes, or until golden.

Remove from the oven and cool on the tray. Store in a dry airtight container until ready to use; the crumbs will keep for up to 1 week.

FOR THE QUINCE CAKES

Grease and line a giant six-hole muffin tin with baking paper.

Combine 250 g (9 oz) of the sugar in a saucepan with 125 ml (4 fl oz/½ cup) water. Bring to the boil and cook for 10–15 minutes, until the toffee is a golden caramel colour.

Pour a small amount of the warm toffee into each muffin mould, enough to cover the bottom. Press 3–4 quince slices into each mould, then set aside to cool.

Meanwhile, preheat the oven to 180°C (355°F).

Cream the butter and remaining sugar in a food processor until light and creamy. Slowly add the eggs one at a time until combined, scraping down the side as needed.

Sift the flour and baking powder into a large bowl and fold in the almond meal. Gently fold the egg mixture into the dry ingredients until combined. Fill the muffin moulds to the tops with the cake batter.

Bake for 25 minutes, or until a skewer inserted comes out clean. Remove from the oven and cool to room temperature in the tin. Remove the cooled cakes by turning them upside down and carefully lifting them out of the tin.

TO SERVE

Put the quince cakes on a baking tray, with the quince portions facing upwards. Reheat in a 175°C (345°F) oven until warm.

Place each cake in the middle of a bowl or plate, then sprinkle some crumble alongside. Top with a generous scoop of almond ice-cream and serve.

SERVES 6

DARK CHOCOLATE DELICE WITH JAFFA SAUCE, RASPBERRY SORBET & PISTACHIO

— Orange zest powder
(page 182), for sprinkling
— Raspberry sorbet (page 202),
to serve

DELICE

— 370 g (13 oz) 65% couverture
chocolate, melted and kept
warm, plus extra melted dark
chocolate, for coating your
12 delice moulds
— 160 g (5½ oz) caster
(superfine) sugar
— 2 eggs
— 4 egg yolks
— 500 ml (17 fl oz/2 cups)
semi-whipped cream
(whipped until just thickened)

CONTINUES OPPOSITE →

This would have to be the Huxtable signature dessert, created by our dessert maestro, Krista Corbett. The flavours are rich but balanced, and it looks amazing too. There was an uproar among the regulars when this dessert was taken off the menu. This recipe makes 12, as it is a lot of work to make just six. You can then leave any uneaten portions in the freezer, but I know they won't last long!

FOR THE DELICE

Thinly coat twelve 105 ml (3½ fl oz) delice moulds with some extra melted chocolate; we use 7 cm x 4 cm (2¾ inch x 1½ inch) diameter half-sphere silicone moulds. Make sure the chocolate coating is as thin as possible, and wipe the edges clean. Cover with baking paper and store in the freezer to set the chocolate.

Place the sugar in a small saucepan with enough water — about 2 tablespoons — to create a wet 'sand' mixture. Brushing down the side of the pan with water as necessary, heat the sugar slowly. When it reaches 115°C (239°F) on a sugar thermometer, begin whisking the eggs and egg yolks on high speed, using an electric mixer.

When the sugar reaches 118°C (244°F), remove the pan from the heat. When the bubbles have subsided, slowly pour the sugar mixture into the whisking egg mixture. Continue whisking until the bottom of the bowl is cold.

Transfer the mixture to a clean, dry bowl. Quickly mix in one-third of the melted chocolate, then fold in the remaining melted chocolate. Working quickly, stir in one-third of the whipped cream, making sure to scrape the bottom of the bowl.

Spoon the mixture into a disposable piping (icing) bag, then pipe into the frozen chocolate-coated moulds, making sure not to leave any air gaps. Using a palette knife, smooth over the tops, to create a completely flat surface.

Store in the freezer until needed; the delice will keep for several days.

Continues opposite →

CONTINUED FROM
PREVIOUS PAGE →

BITTER DARK CHOCOLATE
JAFFA SAUCE

— 55 ml (1¾ fl oz) milk
— 110 ml (4 fl oz) pouring
  (single/light) cream
— 55 ml (1¾ fl oz) liquid glucose
— 30 ml (1 fl oz) Grand Marnier,
  or other orange-flavoured
  brandy liqueur
— 2 oranges, zested with a
  peeler, taking care to avoid the
  white pith
— 165 g (6 oz) dark chocolate,
  chopped

PISTACHIO GARNISH

— 3 tablespoons isomalt
  (see Note)
— 2 tablespoons blanched,
  peeled, toasted and
  chopped pistachio nuts,
  plus extra for sprinkling

•
ISOMALT IS A SUGAR
SUBSTITUTE MADE FROM
BEETROOT (BEETS). IT IS AS
SWEET AS SUGAR, BUT WITH
HALF THE CALORIES, AND
RESISTS CRYSTALLISING.

FOR THE BITTER DARK CHOCOLATE JAFFA SAUCE

Combine the milk, cream, glucose, Grand Marnier and orange zest in a saucepan. Warm over very low heat for 15 minutes, making sure the mixture doesn't reduce.

In a large bowl, combine the chocolate and 110 ml (4 fl oz) water. Pour in the hot milk mixture, whisking constantly until all the chocolate has melted and a shiny, smooth sauce has formed. Leave at room temperature until cool, then strain through a fine sieve, into a container. Cover and store in the fridge; the sauce will keep for several days.

FOR THE PISTACHIO GARNISH

Preheat the oven to 190°C (375°F) and line a large round tray with baking paper. Place the isomalt on the tray and heat in the oven for 5–6 minutes, until dissolved into a syrup.

Remove the tray to a bench. As the syrup cools down, work it with a small palette knife, to allow it to spread into a thin layer on the tray. Once the isomalt has stopped separating and stays as a thin layer, immediately and evenly sprinkle the pistachios over. Cool on the tray to room temperature, then carefully peel off the isomalt.

Store between sheets of baking paper in a well-sealed container in the freezer; the garnish will keep for several days.

TO ASSEMBLE AND SERVE

At least 6 hours before serving, carefully unmould the delices. To defrost, gently place on the inside of the lid of a large plastic container lined with baking paper. Tape some doubled-over paper towel to the inside of the container (to absorb any condensation as the delices defrost), then place over the delices as a 'lid'.

When the delices have defosted, drizzle a line of jaffa sauce along the middle of each plate using a spoon. Place each delice just to one side of the centre, in the middle of the sauce. Sprinkle some extra chopped pistachios over the line of sauce nearest to the middle of the plate. Using your thumb and index finger, gently sprinkle a line of orange zest powder along the jaffa sauce and across the middle of the delice.

Place a scoop of sorbet on top of the pistachios. Finally, place a shard of the pistachio garnish in between the sorbet and delice. It's a lot of work, but it is certainly worth it!

SERVES 12

•
SWEET

RASPBERRY
SORBET

JAFFA
SAUCE

PISTACHIOS

DARK CHOCOLATE
DELICE

BLOOD ORANGE
SORBET

COCONUT
CRUMBLE

PARFAIT

COCONUT PARFAIT WITH BLOOD ORANGE SORBET, MANGO & PAPAYA

- 1 mango, peeled and finely diced
- 1 papaya, peeled and finely diced
- juice of 1 lime
- Lime gel (page 192), to serve
- 100 g (3½ oz) finely shredded roasted coconut
- Blood orange sorbet (page 199), to serve
- shiso cress, to garnish

COCONUT CRUMBLE

- 75 g (2¾ oz/½ cup) plain (all-purpose) flour
- 55 g (2 oz) brown sugar
- ½ teaspoon ground cinnamon
- 90 g (3¼ oz) butter
- 20 g (¾ oz) shredded coconut

PARFAIT

- 4 egg yolks
- 2 eggs
- 150 g (5½ oz) caster (superfine) sugar
- 500 ml (17 fl oz/2 cups) thickened (whipping) cream
- 110 ml (4 fl oz) coconut cream
- 40 ml (1¼ fl oz) Malibu or other coconut-flavoured rum

The refreshing flavours of this lovely summery dessert are perfect at the end of an Asian-style meal. Or any meal to be honest.

FOR THE CRUMBLE

Preheat the oven to 160°C (320°F).

Combine the flour, sugar, cinnamon and butter in a food processor and pulse to a breadcrumb texture. Transfer to a bowl and stir in the coconut. Work the dough until combined. Place between two sheets of baking paper, then roll the dough out to about 3 mm (⅛ inch) thick.

Place the dough on a baking tray, still on the bottom sheet of baking paper. Bake for 11–13 minutes, or until golden brown. Remove from the oven and leave to cool on the tray, then break up to form a crumble texture. Transfer to an airtight container; the crumbs will keep for up to 1 week.

FOR THE PARFAIT

Line a 28 cm (11 inch), 1.5 litre (51 fl oz/6 cup) terrine mould with baking paper. Place the egg yolks and eggs in the bowl of an electric mixer with a whisk attached.

Boil the sugar with a little water until it reaches 120°C (248°F) on a sugar thermometer. Slowly and steadily pour the sugar syrup into the eggs on high speed. Continue whisking for 5 minutes, or until the eggs are fluffy and cool.

While the eggs are whisking, beat the cream, coconut cream and rum together into firm peaks. Fold the whipped cream mixture through the beaten eggs, then pour the mixture into the terrine mould. Freeze for 3 hours, or until set.

TO SERVE

Spread a thick line of crumble across the middle of the serving plates. Remove the terrine from the mould, by giving a little tug on the ends of the baking paper. Transfer to a board, cut into slices about 2.5 cm (1 inch) thick and place over the crumble.

Gently toss the mango, papaya and lime juice together, then arrange over the parfait. Put little dollops of lime gel over the crumble, then sprinkle with the shredded coconut.

Place a scoop of sorbet at one end, garnish with the cress and serve.

SERVES 6–8

SWEET

PORT-BAKED FIGS, CINNAMON CAKE, MAPLE JELLY & FIG-LEAF ICE-CREAM

— Fig-leaf ice-cream (page 200), to serve

MAPLE JELLY

— 250 ml (8½ fl oz/1 cup) maple syrup
— 5 gelatine leaves, soaked in cold water

CINNAMON CAKE

— 150 g (5½ oz) butter
— 180 g (6½ oz/½ cup) honey
— 110 g (4 oz/½ cup) dark brown sugar
— 260 g (9 oz/1¾ cups) plain (all-purpose) flour
— 2 teaspoons baking powder
— 2 tablespoons ground cinnamon
— 2 eggs, lightly beaten

CONTINUES OVERLEAF →

Figs are such a sensual fruit in the way they look and feel in the mouth. This is a great autumnal dessert. You'll be surprised at the flavour that comes out of the fig leaf.

FOR THE MAPLE JELLY

Spray some takeaway containers with cooking oil spray (or use a paper towel dipped in oil), then wipe out with paper towel.

Heat the maple syrup and 250 ml (8½ fl oz/1 cup) water over low heat until the maple syrup has dissolved. Add the gelatine leaves, whisking to dissolve.

Strain through a fine sieve into the containers. Cover and place in the fridge to set for at least 2 hours; the jelly will keep for several days.

FOR THE CINNAMON CAKE

Preheat the oven to 160°C (320°F) and line a loaf (bar) tin with baking paper.

Combine the butter, honey and sugar in a saucepan and heat slowly until a smooth caramel forms. Leave to cool.

Sift the flour, baking powder and cinnamon into a bowl, then make a well in the centre. Add the eggs, then the cooled caramel. Fold together until a smooth batter forms. Pour into the loaf tin and smooth the top with a palette knife.

Bake for 20 minutes, or until a skewer inserted in the middle of the cake comes out clean. Transfer to a wire rack and leave to cool to room temperature.

Using a serrated knife, cut off the crusts, then cut the cake into 2 cm (¾ inch) cubes. Store at room temperature in between sheets of baking paper in dry airtight containers; the cake can be made a day ahead.

Continues overleaf →

SERVE WITH
COFFEE

A GREAT
AUTUMNAL
DESSERT

SWEET

CONTINUED FROM
PREVIOUS PAGES →

PORT-BAKED FIGS

— 100 ml (3½ fl oz) port
— 100 ml (3½ fl oz) red wine
— 2 tablespoons honey
— 55 g (2 oz/¼ cup) caster
   (superfine) sugar
— ½ vanilla bean, split
   lengthways and seeds scraped
— 6 ripe figs, top and bottom
   trimmed, the top of each fig
   lightly scored

CRISP FILO GARNISH

— 2 tablespoons icing
   (confectioners') sugar
— 1 teaspoon ground cinnamon
— 3 sheets filo pastry
— 100 ml (3½ fl oz) melted butter

FOR THE BAKED FIGS

Preheat the oven to 160°C (320°F). Combine the port, wine, honey, sugar and vanilla seeds in a saucepan with 100 ml (3½ fl oz) water. Slowly bring to a simmer, then remove from the heat.

Place the figs in a deep-sided non-stick baking tray. Pour enough of the warm port mixture into the baking tray to reach one-quarter of the way up the figs. Roll the figs in the liquid, then stand them upright. Cover the tray with foil and bake for 10 minutes, or until the figs are just cooked.

Let the figs sit in the liquid for 10 minutes. Remove the foil and leave the figs in the tray to cool to room temperature.

Pour 300 ml (10 fl oz) of the fig liquid into a small saucepan. Cook over low heat for 15 minutes, until the liquid is reduced to a syrup consistency, skimming off any foam that rises to the surface. The syrup will be a lot thicker when it cools, so add a little more liquid from the tray if it is too thick once cooled.

FOR THE CRISP FILO GARNISH

Preheat the oven to 175°C (350°F) and line a tray with baking paper.

Mix the icing sugar and cinnamon together in a small bowl.

Lay one sheet of filo pastry on a bench and, using a pastry brush, completely cover the filo with melted butter. Gently dust the filo with the combined sugar and cinnamon using a fine sieve. Place a second and third sheet of filo over the first, repeating the brushing and dusting process between each layer. Cut the filo into triangles about 3 cm (2 inches) long. Place the triangles onto the baking tray, top with another sheet of baking paper and then place a second baking tray on top to keep them flat while baking. Bake for 8–10 minutes until golden brown. Transfer to a wire rack and leave to cool to room temperature.

TO SERVE

Warm the figs in the oven. Arrange some cake cubes along one side of each plate. Slice each fig in half, then evenly space them among the cake cubes.

Use a teaspoon to place little 'gems' of the maple jelly among the cake cubes. Rest the filo garnish on top. Scoop a generous scoop of ice-cream onto each plate, drizzle with the fig syrup and serve.

SERVES 6

TRIFLE OF POACHED PEACHES, RASPBERRIES, LEMON CURD CREAM & SPARKLING JELLY

- 6 ripe white peaches
- 10 gelatine leaves, soaked in cold water
- 1 quantity Lemon curd cream (page 192)
- 1 Genoise sponge cake (page 190), cut into 2 cm (¾ inch) cubes
- 150 ml (5 fl oz) moscato
- 450 g (1 lb) raspberries

POACHING LIQUID

- zest of 2 lemons, peeled using a vegetable peeler
- zest of 2 limes, peeled using a vegetable peeler
- 6 mint sprigs
- 500 g (1 lb 2 oz) sugar
- 500 ml (17 fl oz/2 cups) white wine

This is a perfect summer trifle to finish off an alfresco lunch. So fresh and light — and a good excuse to open another bottle of bubbles! The trifle is best made a few hours ahead, so all the layers and flavours can settle and come together.

TO POACH THE PEACHES

Combine the poaching liquid ingredients and 500 ml (17 fl oz/2 cups) water in a saucepan. Bring to the boil, then reduce the heat.

Cut around the natural seam of the peaches and twist the halves to separate them. Remove the stones, then place the peach halves in the poaching liquid. Cover with a round of baking paper, then place a side plate on top to keep the peaches submerged. Bring the liquid to poaching temperature (just below simmering point — there should be no movement in the liquid, maybe just a few bubbles on the bottom of the pan).

Poach for 20–30 minutes, or until the peaches are just tender. Remove the peaches from the liquid and leave to cool; reserve the liquid for the jelly.

Gently slip the skins off the peaches, then cut each half in half. Transfer the peaches to the fridge.

TO MAKE THE JELLY

Measure out 1 litre (34 fl oz/4 cups) of the reserved peach poaching liquid. Transfer 100 ml (3½ fl oz) to a small saucepan and gently warm.

Dissolve the gelatine in the liquid, then strain back into the remaining liquid and mix well. Pour into a container, then cover and refrigerate for 2 hours, or until set. Once completely set, dice into 1 cm (½ inch) cubes.

TO ASSEMBLE

Place about one-third of the lemon curd cream in the bottom of individual glasses or a glass serving bowl. Add half the diced sponge cake and sprinkle with half the moscato. Next add half the peaches and one-third of the raspberries, arranging them so they can be nicely seen through the glass. Next add half the jelly.

Repeat the process, topping the trifle with a final layer of lemon curd cream and raspberries.

SERVES 6

SRI LANKAN LOVE CAKE WITH TURKISH DELIGHT, MINT ICE-CREAM & GINGER

- 6 pieces candied ginger, thinly sliced
- 60 g (2 oz) chopped roasted cashew nuts
- 40 g (1½ oz/¼ cup) fresh pomegranate seeds
- Mint ice-cream (page 201), to serve
- snipped peppermint cress, to garnish

LOVE CAKE

- 125 g (4½ oz/1 cup) semolina
- 65 g (2¼ oz) unsalted butter, at room temperature
- 5 eggs, separated
- 250 g (9 oz) caster (superfine) sugar
- 100 g (3½ oz) chopped roasted cashew nuts
- 1 tablespoon rosewater
- 1 tablespoon honey
- ⅛ teaspoon lemon zest
- ⅛ teaspoon ground nutmeg
- ¼ teaspoon ground cardamom
- ⅛ teaspoon ground cinnamon
- icing (confectioners') sugar, for dusting

CONTINUES OVERLEAF →

This is an exotic dessert, drawing on Sri Lankan flavours. The semolina cake separates as it cooks and has a beautiful sticky, custardy layer on top. The liquid Turkish delight is so yummy you can just eat it on its own with a spoon! I love the freshness of the mint ice-cream.

FOR THE LOVE CAKE

Preheat the oven to 150°C (300°F). Spray an 18 cm (7 inch) square cake tin with cooking oil spray and line with baking paper.

Place the semolina on a baking tray and heat in the oven for 5 minutes. Transfer to a bowl, then stir in the butter.

In a large bowl, beat the egg yolks and caster sugar together using a hand whisk until light and creamy. Add the semolina mixture and beat until combined. Add the cashews, rosewater, honey, lemon zest and spices and mix together.

In a clean dry bowl, beat the egg whites until they form soft peaks. Fold the egg whites into the cake mixture, then pour into the cake tin.

Bake for 50–60 minutes; if the top starts to get too brown, cover it with foil. This cake is very moist, so do not use the skewer test to check if it's ready; instead, lightly jiggle the cake tin and make sure there is no runny batter.

Remove from the oven and allow the cake to fully cool in the tin. Do not flip it out of the tin, as it's quite sticky and delicate!

When cooled, cut the cake into 18 nice diamonds. Remove from the tin and dust with a little icing sugar.

Continues overleaf →

SWEET

THE SEMOLINA CAKE SEPARATES AS IT COOKS AND HAS A BEAUTIFUL STICKY, CUSTARDY LAYER ON TOP

CONTINUED FROM
PREVIOUS PAGES →

TURKISH DELIGHT SAUCE

- 420 g (15 oz) caster
  (superfine) sugar
- 1 tablespoon lemon juice
- 35 g (1¼ oz) cornflour
  (cornstarch), mixed to a paste
  with 30 ml (1 fl oz) water
- 1 tablespoon pomegranate
  molasses (see Note)
- 1 teaspoon rosewater

FOR THE TURKISH DELIGHT SAUCE

Put the sugar in a saucepan with 250 ml (8½ fl oz/1 cup) water and bring to
the boil. Once the mixture has reached 120°C (248°F) on a sugar thermometer,
add the lemon juice. Cook for 5 minutes, then stir in the cornflour mixture.

Now cook the mixture over low heat until the sauce starts to become
a light caramel. Stir in the pomegranate molasses and rosewater, transfer
to a container and leave to cool.

TO SERVE

Arrange the cake pieces on a tray lined with baking paper
and warm in a 160°C (320°F) oven for 5 minutes.

Smear a generous amount of Turkish delight sauce on
the middle of six plates. Arrange three cake diamonds on
the Turkish delight, with the pointed ends facing towards
each other. Sprinkle the candied ginger, cashews and
pomegranate seeds on top of the exposed Turkish delight.

Place a nice scoop of mint ice-cream where all the cake
points meet. Scatter with the peppermint cress and serve.

SERVES 6

POMEGRANATE
MOLASSES IS A
SWEET/SOUR SYRUP
MADE BY BOILING
AND REDUCING
POMEGRANATE
JUICE. IT IS USED
WIDELY IN MIDDLE
EASTERN COOKERY.

PEANUT BUTTER COOKIES

- 440 g (15½ oz) caster (superfine) sugar
- 500 g (1 lb 2 oz/2 cups) crunchy peanut butter
- 2 eggs
- 2 teaspoons bicarbonate of soda (baking soda)

This recipe was given to me when I worked at Blake's Cafeteria in Melbourne. It is super quick and easy, and gluten free.

Preheat the oven to 165°C (330°F). Line a large baking tray with baking paper.

Place all the ingredients in the bowl of an electric mixer with a paddle attached. Beat on high for 3–4 minutes, or until well combined.

Transfer the mixture to a clean bowl and cover with plastic wrap. Chill in the fridge for 30 minutes, or until the mixture has firmed up.

When the mixture has firmed, roll it into balls about 3 cm (1¼ inches) in diameter. Place on the baking tray, leaving at least 5 cm (2 inches) between the balls. Lightly squash the balls down using the tines of a fork.

Bake for 8–10 minutes, or until golden. The cookies will still be a little soft, but will firm up when cooled.

The cookies can be stored in an airtight container in a cool dark place for several days.

MAKES ABOUT 20

SWEET

SALTED CARAMELS

- 330 g (11½ oz/1½ cups) sugar
- 265 g (9½ oz) golden syrup or treacle
- 1 teaspoon salt flakes, plus extra to garnish
- 300 ml (10 fl oz) thickened (whipping) cream
- 1 vanilla bean, split lengthways and seeds scraped
- 100 g (3½ oz) salted butter

This recipe was given to me by the talented Andrea Reiss, who now has Chez Dré in Melbourne. Her first job in a kitchen was with me at Arintji in 2003, and after working in some of the world's finest restaurants she now has an amazing patisserie café. Salted caramel is one of the 'it' ingredients of the last five years. These are perfect for someone who doesn't want dessert, but just a little sweet bite.

Grease and line a 10 cm x 15 cm (4 inch x 6 inch) baking dish with baking paper.

In a heavy-based saucepan, heat the sugar, golden syrup and salt to 155°C (311°F) on a sugar thermometer.

In a separate saucepan, heat the cream, vanilla pod, vanilla seeds and half the butter.

Carefully add the cream mixture to the caramel mixture — take care as it can spit! Now cook the mixture to 127°C (261°F) on the sugar thermometer.

Remove from the heat and whisk in the remaining butter. Pour into the lined dish and leave to cool completely for 3–4 hours, until set.

Oil a long knife and cut the caramels to your desired size or shape; I like 2 cm (¾ inch) cubes. Sprinkle with extra salt flakes.

Serve as is, or cut 6 cm (2½ inch) squares of clear cellophane and wrap the caramels up like little bonbons, wearing latex gloves so you don't leave fingerprints or stick to the caramels.

MAKES ABOUT 30

SALTED CARAMELS

YOUNG COCONUT
MARSHMALLOWS

PASSIONFRUIT
MARSHMALLOWS

PASSIONFRUIT MARSHMALLOWS

— 200 ml (7 fl oz) passionfruit purée
— 2½ tablespoons powdered gelatine
— 450 g (1 lb) caster (superfine) sugar
— 1 teaspoon lemon juice
— 2 egg whites, at room temperature

Another post-dinner sweet treat with all the flavour, but without the calories of a full serve of dessert!

Combine the passionfruit purée and gelatine and set aside to 'bloom' for 10 minutes.

In a saucepan, dissolve the sugar with the lemon juice and enough water to create a wet 'sand' mixture. Cook, brushing the side of the pan with a wet pastry brush, to 125°C (257°F) on a sugar thermometer.

Remove from the heat and whisk in the passionfruit mixture, stirring to completely dissolve the gelatine.

Whip the egg whites using the whisk attachment of an electric mixer until soft peaks form. Pour the hot passionfruit mixture slowly onto the egg whites and keep beating until doubled in volume. Continue whisking until the egg whites are thick, shiny and cool to touch — the mixture should form soft peaks.

Pour into a greased 20 cm x 24 cm (8 inch x 9½ inch) tray lined with baking paper. Cover with another sheet of baking paper, then leave to set in the fridge for at least 3 hours, or overnight.

Cut into portions using a hot knife, only separating the pieces after you have finished cutting. Store in an airtight container between sheets of baking paper; the marshmallows will keep for up to 1 week.

MAKES 30

YOUNG COCONUT MARSHMALLOWS

— 450 g (1 lb) sugar
— 3 teaspoons liquid glucose
— 200 ml (7 fl oz) coconut water
— 2 egg whites
— 9 gelatine leaves, softened in 140 ml (4½ fl oz) extra coconut water
— toasted shredded coconut, mixed with kaffir lime (makrut) powder (see Note), for coating

Combine the sugar, glucose and coconut water in a saucepan and heat to 127°C (260°F) on a sugar thermometer.

Meanwhile, using the whisk attachment of an electric mixer, beat the egg whites to stiff peaks.

When the sugar mixture has reached the desired temperature, add the gelatine mixture, being careful to avoid being splashed when it bubbles up.

Transfer to a metal jug and slowly pour the mixture into the egg whites while beating; the mixture will thicken and become shiny. Continue to beat for 5–10 minutes, or until the mixture is cool.

Spread into a 20 cm x 24 cm (8 inch x 9½ inch) tray lined with plastic wrap. Cover and leave to set in the fridge for a few hours, or overnight.

Cut into cubes and coat with the coconut and kaffir lime powder. The marshmallows will keep in an airtight container for up to 1 week.

MAKES 24

•
TO MAKE KAFFIR LIME POWDER, DRY SOME FRESH LIME LEAVES IN THE OVEN, THEN RUB THEM THROUGH A FINE SIEVE.

BASICS

AÏOLI

— 4 egg yolks
— 3 teaspoons chardonnay
  vinegar
— 1 tablespoon dijon mustard
— 2 garlic cloves, grated
— 125 ml (4 fl oz/½ cup) olive oil

Place the egg yolks, vinegar, mustard and garlic in a bowl and beat with a hand whisk until combined.

Slowly whisk in the olive oil to form an emulsion. Continue whisking until all the oil has been absorbed and the aïoli has become thick.

Season with salt and ground black pepper and store in the fridge until required; the aïoli will keep for several days.

MAKES ABOUT 250 G (9 OZ/1 CUP)

CHILLI GHERKINS

— 350 ml (12 fl oz) rice vinegar
— 55 g (2 oz/¼ cup) sugar
— 1 red bird's eye chilli, halved
— 1 teaspoon mustard seeds
— 12 baby cucumbers

Bring all the ingredients, except the cucumbers, to the boil in a non-reactive saucepan. Don't stand over the pan and breathe in, or the fumes will burn your nose off!

Remove from the heat and leave to cool completely. Put the cucumbers in a non-reactive container with the pickling liquid and refrigerate for at least 24 hours.

MAKES 12

DASHI STOCK

— 2 pieces dried kombu (dried edible kelp), each about 10 cm (4 inches) long
— 3 dried bonito shavings (see Note)
— 30 ml (1 fl oz) light soy sauce
— 1 tablespoon mirin

Put the kombu in a saucepan with 2 litres (68 fl oz/8 cups) water. Slowly bring to the boil, removing the kombu just before the water starts to boil.

As the water boils, add the bonito and simmer for 30 seconds.

Immediately strain through a fine strainer. Add the soy sauce and mirin.

The stock can be refrigerated for up to 3 days, or frozen in airtight containers for several months.

MAKES ABOUT 2 LITRES (68 FL OZ/8 CUPS)

• SHAVED BONITO, OR KATSUOBUSHI, IS DRIED, FERMENTED AND SMOKED SKIPJACK TUNA, AVAILABLE FROM JAPANESE GROCERS.

DILL OIL

— 6 dill sprigs, stalks trimmed
— 100 ml (3½ fl oz) grapeseed oil
— pinch of citric acid

Reserve a few nice dill tips for garnishing. Bring a saucepan of salted water to the boil, then add the dill and cook for 20–30 seconds. Refresh immediately in iced water. Once cold, remove and drain on paper towel. Use your hands to squeeze as much of the water from the dill as possible.

Finely chop the dill, then place in a blender with the grapeseed oil, citric acid and a pinch of sea salt. Blitz until the oil is very green and has a strong dill flavour. Place in a sieve lined with a coffee filter or very fine muslin (cheesecloth), set over a bowl. Leave to strain in the fridge for about 1 hour. Do not press the mixture through; just let gravity do its thing.

The dill oil is best used within a day or two.

MAKES ABOUT 100 ML (3½ FL OZ)

•
BASICS

HARISSA

- 10 dried chillies
- 1 teaspoon cumin seeds
- ¾ teaspoon coriander seeds
- 1 roasted red capsicum
  (bell pepper), peeled
  and seeded
- 10 red bird's eye chillies
- 2 garlic cloves
- ½ teaspoon sea salt
- 125 ml (4 fl oz/½ cup) olive oil

Soak the dried chillies in hot water for 20 minutes, or until soft. Drain.

Separately toast the cumin seeds and coriander seeds in a dry frying pan over medium heat for a few minutes each time, until fragrant, then tip them into a food processor.

Add the drained chillies, fresh chillies, garlic and salt. Now slowly drizzle in the olive oil, while blitzing to a smooth paste.

Transfer to a clean airtight container; the harissa will keep in the fridge for up to 2 weeks.

MAKES ABOUT 285 G (10 OZ)

HUMMUS

- 200 g (7 oz) dried chickpeas,
  soaked overnight
- pinch of bicarbonate of soda
  (baking soda)
- 2 garlic cloves, crushed
- 1 teaspoon cumin seeds,
  toasted and ground
- 1 teaspoon coriander seeds,
  toasted and ground
- 2 tablespoons tahini
- 100 ml (3½ fl oz) olive oil
- 60 ml (2 fl oz/¼ cup)
  lemon juice

Place the chickpeas and bicarbonate of soda in a saucepan of salted cold water and bring to the boil. Simmer for about 45 minutes to 1 hour, until the chickpeas are tender and almost beginning to break apart. Drain the chickpeas, reserving 1 tablespoon of the cooking liquid.

Place the warm chickpeas in a food processor with the rest of the ingredients and season with salt and pepper. Blitz until a smooth purée is made. Check the seasoning and also the amount of lemon juice and adjust as necessary. Set aside to cool.

Transfer to a clean airtight container; the hummus will keep in the fridge for several days.

MAKES ABOUT 430 G (15 OZ/2 CUPS)

MARINATED OLIVES

— extra virgin olive oil
— olives of your choice
— strips of orange and lemon zest, removed using a vegetable peeler
— bay leaves
— long red chillies, cut into large pieces
— thyme sprigs
— garlic cloves, lightly crushed

Don't throw out the oil once you've used the olives! It's great for dipping bread into, adding to pasta dishes, and myriad other uses.

Start by using roughly equal quantities of olive oil and olives — you'll need enough oil to fully cover your olives.

Pour the olive oil into a saucepan and add some orange and lemon zest, bay leaves, chillies, thyme and garlic, in quantities to suit your taste. Gently warm the oil to infuse the flavours.

Put the olives in a container and pour the warm oil mixture over them. Cover and steep in the refrigerator. The longer you let the olives sit, the better the flavour will be; they can be refrigerated for up to 1 month.

SERVE AS A SNACK

ORANGE ZEST POWDER

— 3 oranges (choose brightly coloured ones)

Preheat the oven to 90°C (195°F). Zest the oranges onto a silicone mat set on a flat baking tray. Spread the zest out evenly.

Bake for 35 minutes, or until the zest is completely dried out and will crumble to a powder in your fingers.

Leave to cool to room temperature, then crumble with your fingers as finely as possible, into a completely dry airtight container. This powder should always be stored with the lid on, because it will absorb moisture readily. Seal the container well; the powder can be stored in a cool dark place for up to 1 week.

MAKES ABOUT 2 TABLESPOONS

PLUM TONKATSU

— 250 g (9 oz) blood plums, halved, stones removed
— 1 green apple, peeled and grated
— 50 ml (1¾ fl oz) worcestershire sauce
— 50 ml (1¾ fl oz) tomato sauce (ketchup)
— 100 ml (3½ fl oz) rice vinegar
— 1 teaspoon mustard powder
— 2 tablespoons brown sugar
— 2 garlic cloves, crushed
— 2 cm (¾ inch) knob fresh ginger, peeled and finely grated
— pinch of ground cloves

Blitz all the ingredients together in a blender.

Transfer to a saucepan and reduce over medium heat for 20 minutes, or until the sauce becomes thick, skimming off any froth that rises to the top. Make sure you stir frequently, as it can stick to the bottom.

Strain and leave to cool. Pour into a clean bottle and seal. The tonkatsu will keep in the refrigerator for up to 1 month.

MAKES ABOUT 500 ML (17 FL OZ/2 CUPS)

TAMARIND WATER

— 100 g (3½ oz) compressed
  seedless tamarind pulp,
  in block form

Place the tamarind in a bowl with 100 ml (3½ fl oz) water. Mash together with
your hands, then leave to sit for 30 minutes, to allow the tamarind to rehydrate.

Push the tamarind pulp through a fine sieve, discarding the fibrous pulp.
The liquid is now ready to use.

(You can make larger quantities of tamarind water if needed; the general rule
is to rehydrate the tamarind paste in an equal quantity of water.)

MAKES ABOUT 145 ML (5 FL OZ)

WAKAME & SESAME SALT

— 2 tablespoons sesame seeds,
  toasted
— 1 tablespoon dried wakame
— 1 teaspoon sea salt

Place the ingredients in a spice grinder and blitz to the consistency of sand.
Don't process for too long or the oil will come out of the sesame seeds and
make a paste.

Transfer to an airtight container; the salt mixture will keep in a cool dark place
for up to 1 month.

MAKES 2-3 TABLESPOONS

XO CHILLI SAUCE

- 4 dried scallops (see Note), soaked in warm water for 2 hours, then drained
- 50 g (1¾ oz) dried shrimp, soaked in warm water for 2 hours, then drained
- 200 g (7 oz) long red chillies, seeded and finely chopped
- 50 g (1¾ oz) fresh ginger, finely chopped
- 50 g (1¾ oz) garlic, peeled and finely chopped
- 2 teaspoons sea salt
- 2 teaspoons sugar
- 300 ml (10 fl oz) vegetable oil
- 3 spring onions (scallions), finely sliced

Put the scallops on a heatproof plate. Place the plate in a bamboo steamer and set over a saucepan or wok of rapidly boiling water. Cover with the steamer lid and steam for 10 minutes.

Remove the scallops from the steamer. While still warm, shred them with your fingers, separating all the fibres.

Pound the shrimp until finely ground using a mortar and pestle, or grind in a spice grinder.

Put all the ingredients, except the spring onion, in a large heavy-based saucepan. Cook over low heat, stirring occasionally, for 45 minutes, or until the sauce loses its raw edge and turns deep red.

Remove from the heat and leave to cool, then stir in the spring onion.

Transfer to a clean bottle and seal. The sauce will keep in the refrigerator for up to 1 week.

MAKES ABOUT 500 ML (17 FL OZ/2 CUPS)

DRIED SCALLOPS ARE ALSO KNOWN AS CONPOY AND HAVE A RICH 'UMAMI' FLAVOUR. YOU'LL FIND THEM SOLD IN PACKETS AT ASIAN GROCERS.

HUXTABLE BREAD

- 900 g (2 lb/6 cups) plain (all-purpose) flour, plus extra for dusting
- 1 heaped tablespoon sea salt, plus 1 tablespoon extra, for sprinkling
- 1 tablespoon fresh yeast, or 2 teaspoons (7 g) dried yeast
- 600 ml (20½ fl oz) warm water
- 2 tablespoons extra virgin olive oil

Bread is one of the great simple pleasures in life. It unifies all cultures and brings people together to break it. For me there are few better smells than fresh bread out of the oven. Warm, just-baked bread with lots of excellent butter is heaven!

Mix the flour and salt together in a large bowl.

Whisk the yeast and water together, then pour into the dry ingredients. Mix together, then turn out onto a lightly floured bench and knead until a smooth ball forms.

Place in a clean bowl dusted with a little flour. Cover with plastic wrap and leave to prove in a warm draught-free spot for 1 hour, or until doubled in size.

Knock back the dough by punching it lightly, then shape into two or three loaves. Place on a tray lined with baking paper. Cover with a cloth and put the loaves in a warm place to prove for a second time, until doubled in size again.

Meanwhile, preheat the oven to 220°C (430°F).

Brush the loaves with the olive oil and sprinkle the extra salt over the top. Bake for 20 minutes, or until a dark golden crust has formed.

Remove from the oven and place on a rack to cool. The bread is best eaten within a day or so.

MAKES 2–3 LOAVES (YOU CHOOSE THE SIZE)

HUXTABLE
BREAD

MARINATED
OLIVES

SESAME WAFERS

- 85 g (3 oz) butter
- 85 g (3 oz) caster (superfine) sugar
- 40 g (1½ oz) corn syrup
- 25 ml (¾ fl oz) milk
- 50 g (1¾ oz) black sesame seeds
- 50 g (1¾ oz) white sesame seeds

Preheat the oven to 160°C (320°F) and line a baking tray with baking paper.

Combine the butter, sugar, corn syrup and milk in a small saucepan. Warm over low heat, stirring once or twice, until the sugar has completely dissolved. Remove from the heat and stir in the sesame seeds. Cool in the refrigerator for about 1 hour, or until firm.

Roll the mixture into small balls, press slightly and place on the baking tray. Bake for 10 minutes, or until golden brown. Allow to harden and cool on the tray, then carefully remove with a spatula.

Place in an airtight container, with sheets of baking paper between each layer. Store in the freezer to protect against humidity and use within a day.

MAKES ABOUT 50

VANILLA TUILES

- 100 g (3½ oz) plain (all-purpose) flour
- 150 g (5½ oz) icing (confectioners') sugar
- 4 egg whites
- 45 ml (1½ fl oz) melted butter
- ½ vanilla bean, split lengthways and seeds scraped

Preheat the oven to 160°C (320°F) and line a baking tray with a non-stick baking mat or baking paper.

Sift the flour and icing sugar together. Slowly fold in the egg whites, then fold in the melted butter and vanilla seeds. Chill for 30 minutes, until spreadable.

Use a palette knife to smear random shapes of even thickness on the baking tray. Bake for 10 minutes, or until golden and crisp.

Leave on the baking tray to cool, then break to your desired size. Can be made a day in advance, but must be stored in an airtight container until required.

MAKES ABOUT 20, DEPENDING ON SIZE

SHORTBREAD

— 155 g (5½ oz) sugar
— 300 g (10½ oz/2 cups) plain (all-purpose) flour
— pinch of sea salt
— 210 g (7½ oz) cold butter, diced

Combine the sugar, flour and salt. Place the butter in a food processor with half the flour mixture. Pulse until just combined, scraping down the side as needed. Add the remaining flour mixture and pulse until it resembles breadcrumbs.

Tip the mixture into a bowl and lightly knead to form a dough. Divide into two portions, cover with plastic wrap and rest in the fridge for at least 3 hours.

Remove the dough from the fridge 30 minutes before you want to use it. Roll the dough out to about 5 mm (¼ inch thick) between two sheets of baking paper, then place back in the fridge, still between the paper, to rest for at least 30 minutes.

Preheat the oven to 160°C (320°F) and line a baking tray with baking paper. Peel the top paper layer from the dough, then use a 10 cm (4 inch) ring cutter to cut out 10 discs. Place on the baking tray and prick each with a fork a few times. Bake for 10–12 minutes, or until just cooked and very lightly golden.

Leave on the trays to cool, then remove once set. Store in an airtight container in a cool dark place; the shortbread will keep for several days.

MAKES 10

GENOISE SPONGE

- softened butter, for greasing
- 4 eggs
- 125 g (4½ oz) caster (superfine) sugar
- 125 g (4½ oz) plain (all-purpose) flour, sifted, plus extra for dusting
- 30 g (1 oz) butter, melted and cooled

Genoise sponge is one of the absolute basics in the pastry kitchen. For a long time I have used a recipe inspired by Michel Roux, considered to be one of the true pastry masters. Traditionalists make the cake by hand, but you can use an electric mixer if you like. My tip for folding in the flour is to be firm and quick — too much playing with the batter will result in a flat cake!

Preheat the oven to 190°C (375°F). Butter and lightly flour a 20 cm (8 inch) square cake tin.

Place the eggs and sugar in the bowl of an electric mixer with a whisk attached. Beat on high for 7–8 minutes, or until the mixture is very light and fluffy and forms a 'ribbon' when you lift the whisk.

Gently scatter the flour over and fold until combined, without being too rough. Drizzle in the melted butter and fold it through well, without overworking the batter.

Pour the batter into the cake tin and bake for 30 minutes. To check if the sponge is done, lightly press the top — there should be some resistance. A skewer inserted into the centre of the cake should also come out clean.

Remove from the oven and leave to cool in the tin for about 10 minutes. When cool enough to handle, carefully turn out onto a wire rack to cool completely.

Once completely cooled, the cake can be wrapped in plastic wrap and stored in an airtight container in a cool dark place for several days, or refrigerated for up to 1 week.

MAKES 1 SQUARE 20 CM (8 INCH) CAKE

CHOCOLATE GENOISE SPONGE

— softened butter, for greasing
— 4 eggs
— 125 g (4½ oz) caster (superfine) sugar
— 75 g (2¾ oz/½ cup) plain (all-purpose) flour, plus extra for dusting
— 50 g (1¾ oz) unsweetened cocoa powder
— 30 g (1 oz) butter, melted and cooled

Preheat the oven to 190°C (375°F). Butter and lightly flour a 20 cm (8 inch) square cake tin.

Place the eggs and sugar in the bowl of an electric mixer with a whisk attached. Beat on high for 7–8 minutes, or until the mixture is very light and fluffy and forms a 'ribbon' when you lift the whisk.

Sift the flour and cocoa powder together. Gently scatter the mixture over the batter and fold until combined, without being too rough. Drizzle in the melted butter and fold it through well, without overworking the batter.

Pour the batter into the cake tin and bake for 30 minutes. To check if the sponge is done, lightly press the top — there should be some resistance. A skewer inserted into the centre of the cake should also come out clean.

Remove from the oven and leave to cool in the tin for about 10 minutes. When cool enough to handle, carefully turn out onto a wire rack to cool completely.

Once completely cooled, the cake can be wrapped in plastic wrap and stored in an airtight container in a cool dark place for several days, or refrigerated for up to 1 week.

MAKES 1 SQUARE 20 CM (8 INCH) CAKE

LEMON CURD CREAM

- 250 g (9 oz) sugar
- zest and juice of 6 lemons
- 5 eggs
- 2 gelatine leaves, soaked in cold water
- 150 g (5½ oz) cold butter, diced
- 500 ml (17 fl oz/2 cups) cream, softly whipped

Rub the sugar and lemon zest together in a bowl and set aside for 10 minutes.

Place in a saucepan with the lemon juice and eggs and whisk together well. Cook over medium heat for 10 minutes, or until the mixture reaches 80°C (175°F) on a sugar thermometer.

Remove from the heat, then whisk in the gelatine. Pass the mixture through a sieve, into a large bowl, and leave to cool slightly. Slowly whisk in the butter until well combined, then cover and chill in the fridge.

Using a hand whisk, beat the cold lemon curd. Gently fold the cream through, then refrigerate until required. The cream is best used the day it is made.

MAKES 1 LITRE

LEMON OR LIME GEL

- 100 g (3½ oz) caster (superfine) sugar
- 1½ teaspoons agar agar powder
- 100 ml (3½ fl oz) lemon or lime juice, strained

Combine the sugar and agar agar in a saucepan with 100 ml (3½ fl oz) water. Set aside for 15 minutes to allow the agar agar to soften.

Stirring constantly, slowly bring the mixture to a simmer. Stir over medium heat for 10–15 minutes, or until the agar agar has completely dissolved. It should be completely smooth and you should not be able to see any grains.

Cool to room temperature, then whisk in the lemon or lime juice. Pass through a fine strainer, into a container. Cover and set in the fridge for a few hours.

Once set, blitz in a blender on high speed until smooth and glossy, scraping down the side as necessary. Taste the gel and add more lemon or lime juice or sugar if needed. Pour into a clean jar, seal and refrigerate until required. The gel will keep in the refrigerator for up to 2 weeks.

MAKES ABOUT 1 CUP

POACHED QUINCE

— 750 g (1 lb 11 oz) sugar
— 1½ cinnamon sticks
— 3 star anise
— zest of 1½ oranges, removed using a vegetable peeler
— 3 quinces

Pour 1 litre (34 fl oz/4 cups) water into a saucepan. Add the sugar, cinnamon stick, star anise and orange zest and bring to the boil.

Peel, core and quarter the quinces. Add them to the poaching liquid and reduce the heat to low.

Cover with a round of baking paper. Cook for 30–40 minutes, or until the quince is soft. Remove from the heat and leave to cool in the liquid. Refrigerate until required; the quince can be made up to a week in advance and will keep for up to 2 weeks.

MAKES 3 POACHED QUINCES

POACHED RHUBARB

— 500 g (1 lb 2 oz) rhubarb, washed and cut into 3 cm (1¼ inch) batons
— 250 g (9 oz) caster (superfine) sugar
— zest and juice of 1 blood orange

Bring a saucepan of water to poaching temperature (just below simmering point — there should be no movement in the water, maybe just a few bubbles on the bottom of the pan).

Toss the rhubarb together in a bowl with the sugar and orange zest and juice, then transfer the whole mixture to a zip-lock bag. Remove as much air as possible from the bag before sealing it.

Place the bag in the poaching water and cook for 45–50 minutes, or until the rhubarb is just tender. Remove from the water and immediately cool in an iced water bath. Refrigerate until required; the rhubarb will keep for up to 1 week.

MAKES ABOUT 750 G (1 LB 11 OZ/3 CUPS)

RHUBARB CRISPS

— 2 thick rhubarb batons, each 5 cm (2 inches) long, washed
— 125 ml (4 fl oz/½ cup) liquid glucose

Peel the rhubarb with a sharp vegetable peeler to create thin strips.

Heat the glucose in a small saucepan. One by one, dip the rhubarb strips into the hot glucose, until wilted. Remove with a fork and drain on paper towel.

Dry well, then place the rhubarb strips on a sheet of baking paper.

Dehydrate the rhubarb for 1½–2 hours in a preheated 90°C (195°F) oven for 10–15 minutes, or for about 6 hours in a food dehydrator on high, until crisp.

Leave to cool, then store between sheets of baking paper in a completely dry, well-sealed container. The crisps will keep in a cool dark place for several days.

MAKES ABOUT 50 CRISPS

RHUBARB JAM

— 500 g (1 lb 2 oz) rhubarb, cleaned and chopped into 1 cm (½ inch) pieces
— 300 g (10½ oz) caster (superfine) sugar
— zest and juice of 1 blood orange
— ½ vanilla bean, split lengthways and seeds scraped

Combine all the ingredients, including the vanilla pod, in a non-stick saucepan. Cook over very low heat, stirring occasionally, for about 1 hour, or until the mixture is thick and jam-like.

To test if the jam is ready, dollop a small amount into a ramekin and place in the freezer until cold. If the jam is thick and sticky when cold, it is ready.

Remove the vanilla pod. Pour the jam into warm sterilised jars and cool to room temperature. Store in the refrigerator for up to 1 month.

MAKES ABOUT 930 G (2 LB 1 OZ/3 CUPS)

STRAWBERRY CRISPS

— 100 g (3½ oz) firm strawberries

Slice the strawberries thinly and place on a sheet of baking paper.

Dehydrate the strawberries for 1½–2 hours in a preheated 90°C (195°F) oven for 20–25 minutes, or for about 8 hours in a food dehydrator on high, until crisp.

Leave to cool, then store between sheets of baking paper in a completely dry, well-sealed container. The crisps will keep in a cool dark place for several days.

MAKES ABOUT 50 CRISPS

SUGAR SYRUP

— 500 g (1 lb 2 oz) sugar

Put the sugar in a saucepan with 500 ml (17 fl oz/2 cups) water and bring to the boil. Reduce the heat and simmer gently until the sugar has dissolved, being careful not to let the water level reduce.

Leave to cool, then store in an airtight container in the fridge until required. The sugar syrup will keep for several weeks.

MAKES ABOUT 1 LITRE (34 FL OZ/4 CUPS)

DOUGH HOOK

STRAINERS

BRUSH

CLEAVER

GRATER

TONGS

TURNERS

PEELER

SPATULAS

WHISKS

PASTRY BRUSHES

NUTCRACKER

SPATULA

TENDERISER

GRATER

METAL SPOONS

ALMOND ICE-CREAM

- 8 egg yolks
- 30 ml (1 fl oz) liquid glucose
- 250 ml (8½ fl oz/1 cup) pouring (single/light) cream
- 100 g (3½ oz) sugar
- 250 ml (8½ fl oz/1 cup) milk
- Amaretto or other almond-flavoured liqueur, to taste
- 80 g (2¾ oz/½ cup) toasted, chopped blanched almonds

Whisk the egg yolks in a bowl with the glucose.

Scald the cream, sugar and milk in a small saucepan over medium heat. Pour the cream mixture over the egg yolks, whisking constantly until combined.

Pour the mixture back into a clean saucepan and stir constantly over low heat until the mixture is thick and coats the back of the spoon.

Pour immediately into a bowl set over an iced water bath and stir until cool.

Add the liqueur to taste, then churn in an ice-cream machine according to the manufacturer's instructions. Fold the almonds through, then place in the freezer for a few hours to set. The ice-cream will keep in the freezer for about 1 week.

MAKES ABOUT 600 ML (20½ FL OZ)

BLOOD ORANGE SORBET

- 500 ml (17 fl oz/2 cups) blood orange juice, strained
- 110 g (4 oz) caster (superfine) sugar
- 20 g (¾ oz) powdered glucose

Heat 250 ml (8½ fl oz/1 cup) of the orange juice in a saucepan. Add the sugar and glucose and heat until the sugar and glucose have dissolved. Stir in the remaining orange juice and store in the fridge overnight to chill.

The next day, churn in an ice-cream machine according to the manufacturer's instructions, then return to the freezer for a few hours to firm up. The sorbet will keep in the freezer for about 1 week.

MAKES ABOUT 600 ML (20½ FL OZ)

COCONUT SORBET

- 500 ml (17 fl oz/2 cups) full-cream milk
- 250 g (9 oz) caster (superfine) sugar
- 2 teaspoons liquid glucose
- 100 g (3½ oz) desiccated (shredded) coconut
- 500 ml (17 fl oz/2 cups) coconut cream

The sorbet recipe is from my good friend Nick Holloway, who has a restaurant called Nu Nu in Palm Cove, Queensland.

Heat the milk, sugar and desiccated coconut in a saucepan to just below boiling point — do not allow to boil. Remove from the heat and leave to stand for 10–15 minutes.

Stir in the glucose and coconut cream. Strain through a fine sieve and squeeze to extract all of the juice from the solids. Refrigerate the mixture overnight.

Churn in an ice-cream machine according to the manufacturer's instructions, then place in the freezer for a few hours to firm up — the sorbet should be stretchy and chewy. The sorbet will keep in the freezer for about 1 week.

MAKES ABOUT 1 LITRE (34 FL OZ/4 CUPS)

FIG-LEAF ICE-CREAM

- 8 egg yolks
- 50 ml (1¾ fl oz) liquid glucose
- 250 ml (8½ fl oz/1 cup) milk
- 250 ml (8½ fl oz/1 cup) pouring (single/light) cream
- 6 large fig leaves, washed and sliced
- 75 g (2¾ oz) sugar
- ½ vanilla bean, split lengthways and seeds scraped
- 2 strips lemon zest, white pith removed

Whisk the egg yolks and glucose in a large bowl.

Combine the milk, cream, fig leaves, sugar and vanilla in a saucepan and slowly bring to just below boiling point. Remove from the heat and slowly incorporate the milk mixture into the egg yolks, whisking constantly.

Pour back into a clean saucepan and stir over very low heat for 10–12 minutes, until the mixture coats the back of the spoon. Strain into a bowl set over an iced water bath and stir in the lemon zest.

Cool to room temperature, then cover and refrigerate overnight.

The next day, churn in an ice-cream machine to a soft-serve consistency, according to the manufacturer's instructions. Place in the freezer for a few hours to set. The ice-cream will keep in the freezer for about 1 week.

MAKES ABOUT 600 ML (20½ FL OZ)

MANGO SORBET

- 1 heaped tablespoon liquid glucose
- 300 ml (10 fl oz) Sugar syrup (see Basics)
- 2 large mangoes, puréed and passed through a sieve, or 500 g (1 lb 2 oz) mango purée
- juice of 1 lime

Dissolve the glucose in a small amount of the sugar syrup over low heat. Remove from the heat and stir in the mango purée and lime juice.

Strain through a fine strainer and taste to adjust the sweetness and acidity. Refrigerate overnight.

The next day, churn in an ice-cream machine according to the manufacturer's instructions. Place in the freezer for a few hours to set. The sorbet will keep in the freezer for about 1 week.

MAKES ABOUT 500 ML (17 FL OZ/2 CUPS)

MINT ICE-CREAM

- 250 ml (8½ fl oz/1 cup) pouring (single/light) cream
- 250 ml (8½ fl oz/1 cup) milk
- 100 g (3½ oz) sugar
- 6 mint sprigs, plus an extra handful of leaves for churning
- 8 egg yolks
- 2 teaspoons liquid glucose

Combine the cream, milk, sugar and mint sprigs in a saucepan and bring to a simmer. Set aside and leave to infuse for 45 minutes, then strain into a clean saucepan. Gently heat up the infusion.

Whisk the egg yolks in a bowl with the glucose. Pour the warm cream mixture over the egg yolk mixture and whisk to combine.

Pour back into a clean saucepan and stir over very low heat for 10–12 minutes, until the mixture coats the back of the spoon. Strain through a sieve into a bowl set over an iced water bath and stir frequently until cooled. Place in a container and chill overnight in the fridge.

The next day, finely chop up the extra handful of mint leaves and stir them through the ice-cream base. Churn in an ice-cream machine according to the manufacturer's instructions, then place in the freezer for a few hours to set. The ice-cream will keep in the freezer for about 1 week.

MAKES ABOUT 700 ML (23½ FL OZ)

RASPBERRY SORBET

- 500 g (1 lb 2 oz) frozen raspberries
- 1 heaped tablespoon liquid glucose
- 500 ml (17 fl oz/2 cups) Sugar syrup (see Basics)
- juice of 1 lemon

Place the frozen raspberries in a large saucepan and thaw over low heat.

In a small saucepan, dissolve the glucose over low heat with a small amount of sugar syrup. Add the mixture to the raspberries and blitz in a food processor.

Strain the mixture through a fine sieve, removing all the seeds. Skim off any foam that rises to the top and leave to cool.

Add the lemon juice through a sieve, then taste to adjust the sweetness and acidity. Let the mixture sit overnight in the fridge.

The next day, churn in an ice-cream machine according to the manufacturer's instructions. Place in the freezer for a few hours to set. The sorbet will keep in the freezer for about 1 week.

MAKES ABOUT 1 LITRE (34 FL OZ/4 CUPS)

STRAWBERRY SORBET

— 500 g (1 lb 2 oz) fresh
  strawberries, washed, hulled
  and halved; alternatively use
  frozen strawberries
— 115 g (4 oz/½ cup) caster
  (superfine) sugar
— 35 g (1¼ oz) powdered
  glucose
— juice of ½ lemon

Blitz the strawberries well in a food processor and pass through a fine strainer. Pour half the strawberry purée into a saucepan and add the sugar and glucose. Stir well over low heat until the sugar has dissolved and the mixture just begins to boil.

Cool to room temperature, then whisk in the remaining strawberry purée and the lemon juice. Pass through a fine strainer and chill.

Churn in an ice-cream machine according to the manufacturer's instructions. Place in the freezer for a few hours to set. The sorbet will keep in the freezer for about 1 week.

MAKES ABOUT 600 ML (20½ FL OZ)

YOGHURT SORBET

— 25 ml (¾ fl oz) liquid glucose
— 250 ml (8½ fl oz/1 cup)
  Sugar syrup (see Basics)
— 375 g (13 oz/1½ cups)
  plain yoghurt
— juice of ½ lemon
— ½ vanilla bean, split
  lengthways and seeds scraped

In a small saucepan, dissolve the glucose in a small amount of the sugar syrup, then leave to cool.

Combine all the ingredients in a large bowl and whisk well. Strain through a fine sieve into a bowl. Cover and refrigerate the sorbet overnight.

Taste to adjust the acidity and sweetness, then churn in an ice-cream machine according to the manufacturer's instructions. Place in the freezer for a few hours to set. The sorbet will keep in the freezer for about 1 week.

MAKES ABOUT 700 ML (23½ FL OZ)

HUXTABLE,
SMITH STREET
FITZROY

INDEX

CHILLIES

Ceviche of scallops, octopus
  & snapper with chilli & lime 53
Chilli garlic dipping sauce 26
Chilli gherkins 178
Chilli, ginger & black bean
  dressing 34
Chilli pineapple 48
Chilli smoked mussels with aïoli
  & pickled shallot 38
Chipotle & lime crème fraîche 118
Chipotle sauce 119
Green papaya, chilli & peanut
  salad 56
Jalapeño & cheddar croquettes 23
Jalapeño & Thai basil mayo 19
Palm sugar & chilli dressing 103
Rice flour-crusted oyster po' boy
  with sriracha mayo 28
Roasted shallot & chilli dressing 106
Southern fried chicken ribs
  & jalapeño mayo 36
XO chilli sauce 185

Chipotle & lime crème fraîche 118
Chipotle sauce 119

CHOCOLATE

Cherry, pistachio & chocolate
  trifle 143
Chocolate Genoise sponge 191
Dark chocolate delice with
  jaffa sauce, raspberry sorbet
  & pistachio 158–9
Dark/white chocolate fudge 154
Silken chocolate mousse
  with marcona almonds
  & raspberry sauce 138
White chocolate panna cotta
  with salted caramel ganache
  & raspberries 151

Cinnamon cake 164
Cinnamon crumble 156

CITRUS

Blood orange sorbet 199
Citrus crumbs 147
Lemon crème fraîche 20
Lemon curd cream 192
Lemon yoghurt 12
Lemon or lime gel 192
Lemongrass & lime dressing 102
Mandarin crème brûlée with
  cardamom langues de chat 144
Orange blossom custard 142
Orange zest powder 182
Smoked pork cheek with coconut
  sauce, finger lime & lychees 100

COCONUT

Coconut crumble 163
Coconut panna cotta with lychee
  salad & mango sorbet 155
Coconut parfait with blood orange
  sorbet, mango & papaya 163
Coconut prawn salad with rice
  noodles, lychees & cashew
  praline 71
Coconut sauce (tom kha) 100
Coconut sorbet 199
Young coconut marshmallows 175

CORN

Corn purée 33
Steamed crab & corn rice noodle
  rolls with XO chilli sauce 33
Sweet corn & macaroni cheese
  with smoked mozzarella
  & chipotle 119
Warm salad of sweet corn
  & black beans with chipotle
  & lime crème fraîche 118

CRAB

Steamed crab & corn rice noodle
  rolls with XO chilli sauce 33
XO buns with crab & jalapeño
  & Thai basil mayo 19

Crème fraîche cheesecake with
  strawberries, citrus crumbs
  & strawberry sorbet 147–8
Crisp filo logs of lamb puttanesca
  with lemon yoghurt 12
Crisp king salmon tail with pomelo,
  peanut & chilli salad 77
Crumbed oysters with pickled
  plum tartare 14
cucumber, Pickled 20, 64
Cured ocean trout with black
  vinegar & ginger 27

CURRY

Red curry dressing 48
Wagyu & green peppercorn
  curry with coconut, shallot
  & lime leaf 92

CUSTARDS

Orange blossom custard 142
Pistachio custard 143
Yuzu custard 65

D

daikon, Soy 35
Dark chocolate delice with
  jaffa sauce, raspberry sorbet
  & pistachio 158–9
Dashi mushrooms 93
Dashi-poached eggs with confit
  salmon & sesame spinach 50
Dashi stock 179

DESSERTS

Banana fritters with coconut
  sorbet, rum caramel & sesame
  wafers 149
Cherry, pistachio & chocolate
  trifle 143
Coconut panna cotta with lychee
  salad & mango sorbet 155
Coconut parfait with blood orange
  sorbet, mango & papaya 163

INDEX

INDEX

INDEX

U

Upside-down quince cakes with
   cinnamon crumble & almond
   ice-cream 156

V

Vanilla anglaise 153
Vanilla tuiles 188
Veal tartare with soft-boiled egg
   & brioche soldiers 85

W

Wagyu & green peppercorn
   curry with coconut, shallot
   & lime leaf 92
Wagyu beef tataki with roasted
   shallot & chilli dressing
   & toasted rice 106
Wakame & sesame salt 183
Warm salad of sweet corn
   & black beans with chipotle
   & lime crème fraîche 118
Wasabi, yuzu & sesame dressing 47
White chocolate panna cotta
   with salted caramel ganache
   & raspberries 151

X

XO buns with crab & jalapeño
   & Thai basil mayo 19
XO chilli sauce 184

Y

YOGHURT
Harissa yoghurt 114
Lemon yoghurt 12
Yoghurt sorbet 203

Young coconut marshmallows 175
Yuzu custard 65
Yuzu mustard 93

Z

zucchini: Baby carrots with zucchini,
   goat's curd, pomegranate
   & tarragon dressing 110

THANKS

The biggest thanks go to my wife Leah and my two beautiful girls Grace and Maddie. You are my constant support and inspiration, thanks for letting me test ideas on you and always being there to fill my batteries up with love when tired. Without you three none of this would be possible, I love you all with all of my heart xxx.

Mum, Dad, Aunty Prit, Ade and Ange: thanks for always encouraging and believing in me. Though we're not often together, you are all always in my mind and heart.

Grandma and Fath: For always pushing me to be the best I could be and constantly telling me that I could do anything I wanted. Your endless love is still in my heart.

Angus Campbell and all of the instructors at Grand Rapids Community College: you all gave me the foundation to succeed in this industry, which I love so much. Thanks for putting me on the right path.

Andrew Blake and Jacques Reymond et Famille: the years I spent with you prepared me for the big bad world of restaurant ownership. Thanks for always being there and giving me advice when needed.

Dante Ruaine and Jeff Wong: thanks for taking the plunge with me. Here's to a happy and healthy friendship and partnership for many years to come.

Jenny, Krista, Nikki, Matt, Bridget and all of the other chefs who have contributed to what Huxtable is. Jenny, without you this would not be possible and I am truly grateful for all of your hard work and dedication. You're a star.

Shar and all of the Huxtable front of house staff: thanks for looking after the people on the other side of the pass!

To the amazing Hardie Grant team who gently popped my cookbook cherry: Paul McNally for giving me the opportunity, Hannah Koelmeyer for your guidance, Chris Middleton for the amazing photography, Vicki Valsamis for your wicked styling and humour, Katri Hilden for your careful editing, and Suzy Tuxen, Emily Fitts and Cassie Brock from A Friend of Mine for the awesome design!

**PUBLISHED IN 2014
BY HARDIE GRANT BOOKS**

HARDIE GRANT BOOKS (AUSTRALIA)
Ground Floor, Building 1
658 Church Street
Richmond, Victoria 3121
www.hardiegrant.com.au

HARDIE GRANT BOOKS (UK)
Dudley House, North Suite
34–35 Southampton Street
London WC2E 7HF
www.hardiegrant.co.uk

A Cataloguing-in-Publication entry is available from the catalogue
of the National Library of Australia at www.nla.gov.au
Huxtabook
ISBN: 9781742707037

PUBLISHING DIRECTOR: Paul McNally
PROJECT EDITOR: Hannah Koelmeyer
EDITOR: Katri Hilden
DESIGN MANAGER: Heather Menzies
DESIGNER: A Friend of Mine
PHOTOGRAPHER: Chris Middleton
STYLIST: Vicki Valsamis
PRODUCTION MANAGER: Todd Rechner

Colour reproduction by Splitting Image Colour Studio
Printed and bound in China by 1010 Printing International Limited

Find this book on **Cooked.**
cooked.com.au
cooked.co.uk